DOWN IN JERSEY

Down in Jersey

An Affectionate Narrative

by EARL SCHENCK MIERS

RUTGERS UNIVERSITY PRESS

New Brunswick, New Jersey

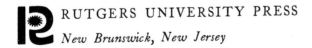

Library of Congress Cataloging in Publication Data

Miers, Earl Schenck, 1910–1972.
  Down in Jersey.

  1. New Jersey—History—Anecdotes, facetiae,
satire, etc.   I.   Title.
F134.6.M53   917.49   73–4365
ISBN 0–8135–0753–7

Contents

DOWN IN JERSEY

Prologue

*My object was not so much to entertain our audience,
as to awaken in the pupils . . . a wholesome interest
in the history of their own locality, to impart to them
the beginnings of that historic lore of which this is so
rich a field, and to arouse and strengthen in them, so
far as possible, the right kind of family and neighborhood pride.*

Susan M. Fillips, teacher *
Stelton Grammar School

The year was 1909. The youth and energy of Miss Fillips
bounced her along to the one-room schoolhouse where she
presided. She was strong-minded and stout-hearted and as
dedicated to teaching as any clergyman to his ecclesiastical
calling. She was not without her eccentricities—for that age,
at any rate—among them her obsession with simplified spell-
ing. Through warm weeks, as spring passed and rabbits
played in the tall grass beyond the open windows, her voice
insisted that "thru" was all anyone needed for "through,"
that the final "e" was nonsensical on a word like "preserv,"
and that "postoffis" for "post office" was natural and under-
standable.

* The quotation is from the Introduction by Susan M. Fillips to *Bits of
History,* a rare pamphlet, published in 1910, and lent to the author by Miss
Margaret Drake. All indented material in *Down in Jersey* relating to the
Class of 1909 at Stelton Grammar School is drawn from this pamphlet.

3

Neither squawking blue jays nor noisy woodpeckers silenced her. Bees that buzzed in the windows would buzz out in time. Of course there were flies—there were always flies —and students killed them and kicked them under the desk for she would sweep the room afterward. Only one occurrence forced her into belligerent muteness—the clanking of the train with the funnel of its engine spewing red-hot cinders and the clanging of the engineer's bell as though he and Miss Fillips were carrying on a private affair (which certainly was not the case). Once the sparks from an engine burned a hole in the roof, and, as might have been expected, the board of education took its own sweet time repairing it. When rain fell the dauntless Miss Fillips placed a bucket under the hole and continued her lessons.

Sometimes Stelton was called Piscataway and sometimes Baptist Roads (today it is a section of Edison). In the first decade of the twentieth century the one-room schoolhouse was surrounded by farm land stretching toward the Watchung Mountains, whose sharp but shadowy cliffs gave Plainfield its original name of Blue Hills. The red buds of maples were signs of burgeoning spring; onion grass left a taste in the milk, and the cows, like the people, revealed their seasonal laziness by lying under protective willows along the banks of the brooks. Butterflies fluttered across the green meadows. The houses were well kept, and some families had settled in the region over two centuries ago. They were proud of their homes, their well-groomed horses and cattle and the freshly painted surreys in which they drove to church on the Sabbath. Rare was the child or parent who did not recognize on his clothing the peculiarly pleasant odor that hay, ammonia, manure, leather and horseflesh give a clean barn.

Spring brought a flutter to Miss Fillips as well as to the butterflies. June was commencement time, and new graduation exercises were needed. But the Class of 1909 at Stelton

Grammar School did not fail their teacher. Legend said that Henry Hudson's *Half Moon* had entered Raritan Bay in September of 1609; why, then, should they not narrate three centuries of local history? Miss Fillips was delighted with the suggestion. They would call their program "Bits of History," Miss Fillips, with her penchant for simplification, decided.

With Miss Fillips, only practice, practice, practice could assure perfection. Angrily, arms akimbo, she interrupted her rehearsals while the express to New Brunswick sped by and the engineer clanged his silly bell. Outwardly the resources for Miss Fillips' "Bits of History" appeared slight: "notably Dr. Brown's history of the church at Stelton" and the few books on the history of East Jersey in the New Brunswick Public Library. But Miss Fillips was an excellent teacher, understanding that the emotion and affection which shone through "Bits of History" must come from the proud tales parents had passed on to their children.

It is a pity that Miss Fillips' wisdom could not escape like a genie from a bottle, for with many residents the State carries on a secret love affair. Actually, New Jersey is an enchanting mistress, filled with the charm of changing moods. She can be secretive and surprising, soft and alluring, her meadows aglow with black-eyed Susans and buttercups, her fields aflame with ripening farm produce, and thoroughbred colts romping across hillsides splattered with daisies and thistles. In lacelike patterns waves run up more than a hundred and twenty-five miles of ocean beaches. Her bays and rivers appeal equally to duck hunters and fishermen. Beyond the bluish haze of the cliffs of the Watchungs roll ranges of green and scenic mountains, and hidden in their valleys, like buried treasures, are the steeples of handsome old churches still standing where they were in the bitter years of the Revolution.

Yet New Jersey possesses her streak of witchery, and almost without warning she can turn vengeful and frightening. The pounding surf of hurricanes erodes her seacoast and luxurious mansions crumble and disappear into a tempestuous Atlantic. Black clouds gather over her mountains, thunder rumbles, and jagged arrows of lightning split whole trees. To the south stand the sandy Pines and Barrens, and God alone knows how many unsolved murders are responsible for the parched human bones sometimes turned over by diggers seeking hidden pirate fortunes in this near wilderness.

Eons ago when man was still evolving, dinosaurs left their tracks in the clays of Perth Amboy and marshes of the Musconetcong Valley. Evidences of glaciers have scarred New Jersey in many places—in the unexpected appearance of her western mountains, in full-grown, petrified cedars submerged in her swamps, in the sea islands off Barnegat Bay and Great and Little Egg Harbors. To the north seagoing vessels must be led by pilot boats into upper New York Bay, and to the south a cape, curving into Delaware Bay, reaches forty miles below the Mason and Dixon Line.

Exploring New Jersey, where its scenes and moods can change from day to day and sometimes from hour to hour, is one of the State's best sports. Always there is some quirk of nature, some all-but-forgotten hamlet, some hitherto unseen delight of nature to stir the heart. Boy scouts pitch their tents on its forested mountainsides, where, in fall, the hunters stalk. There are flower trails to travel, bird sanctuaries to explore, and the beaches, always the beaches, the miles and miles of dunes, and ocean-washed sands, and the lighthouses rising toward the heavens.

A car is virtually indispensable. My wife and I agreed almost in unison that our first automobile, a second-hand Ford coupe, should be called "Alfie," in tribute to Governor Alfred Landon, who was opposing Franklin D. Roosevelt in the presidential election of 1936. We never questioned the governor's ability to run, but there was doubt as to how far he could go. Still, we had paid seventy-five dollars for the coupe, a sizable sum for those early post-Depression years, and we expected good behavior. But Alfie was a fine fellow who never disappointed us (except on icy days when he threatened to skid into the Raritan Canal); and when we swapped him for another used car he had increased in value to one hundred dollars.

For a young couple, weekends devoted to searching for the kind of home where you'd like to raise your family can become an obsession. We found our house, finally, on a dead-end street one block long and no farther than a good stone's throw from the one-room Stelton Grammar School, where Miss Fillips had taught the Class of 1909. That building of course had long since disappeared and in time the red brick railroad station also would go. Otherwise when we first saw the area it was a cluster of modest homes backed against overgrown fields that must have brought generations of agony to hay-fever victims.

But the world had begun to turn skittishly on its axis as the mid-century approached. Within a few decades these fields became (a) Camp Kilmer, an embarkation center for World War II, (b) a refuge for escapees from the Hungarian uprising against their Communist oppressors, (c) a billet for the Peace Corps, (d) a training center for the Job Corps (both national and state), (e) an industrial complex, and (f) a college campus. Elsewhere houses sprang up like toadstools in late spring.

Green grass to cut and trees to climb belong to children. And dogs forever yapping at mailmen. And a window smashing as part of a street baseball game. And a basket-

ball bouncing on sidewalk and driveway. And footballs miss-
ing car windows by inches. And sleds crunching in the snow
and battles raging between icy forts. And commuters returning after dark and screaming bloody murder as they step
on some child's forgotten roller skate.

One day you suddenly miss a child who has been part of
the daily scene for years. "Donald's in Hong Kong," his
mother says. "He's working for the Associated Press."

All at once, with a blink of your eyes, you realize that one
day they will all be gone, including your own, bringing you
in time those punching bags of love called grandchildren,
and a bit weepily but with immense bravery you confess that
you may have passed the middle mark in life.

Then new couples move into the neighborhood. The process begins anew and their children grow like weeds.

Some day the newcomers may realize that they have in-
vaded a territory that mystically will forever belong to Miss
Fillips. They may experience the heat of June days like those
in 1909 as Miss Fillips' heels clicked her way toward the
one-room schoolhouse. The old wooden building reeked with
the steaming warmth, and pigs rooted in the coolness beneath the floor. But Miss Fillips beamed. Her nine narrators were gaining self-confidence, a good speech pace, pleasant tones. For years their minds would expand from the
knowledge they were now acquiring.

The great day arrived. By tradition graduation exercises
of the Stelton Grammar School were held in the old Baptist
Church. Miss Fillips watched with pride the arrival of the
girls in white dresses with ribbons in their hair and the boys
in their blue coats and knickerbockers. By now they seemed
like her own children.

"Miss Fillips," the first narrator said, "I can't get my
cowlick to stay down."

"You'd need bear grease for that."

Suddenly teacher and boy realized the audience had quieted. The very air in the church appeared charged with expectancy. The first narrator stood rigidly stagestruck. His eyes seemed to pop forward.

"You'll be just fine," Miss Fillips whispered. She gave the boy a slight push.

1

The Grandfathers

Master John E. Feller flushed with a sense of apologetic self-consciousness as with a slight stumble he looked down upon the filled pews of the church. The audience became so hushed that when someone suddenly coughed, the sound was like the booming of a cannon. Master Feller, "wearing fringed shoulder sash of red with date [1609] in white, representing Indian period" described the forested wilderness in precolonial times when "no white man's foot had yet trod upon the soil" of "what is now our township." The surrounding "big woods" were filled with "turkeys, foxes, wolves, bears, deer, and other wild animals."

Miss Fillips smiled. She did not believe that students should be taught beyond the accepted limits of their comprehension so that their heads became inflated with unnecessary gasses and floated off to an unknown doom. If Master Feller romanticized the Lenni Lenape's industry, peacefulness and community organization, Miss Fillips did not feel the slightest twitch of guilty conscience.

When Henry Hudson sailed into Raritan Bay in 1609, aboard the *Half Moon* was a mate, Robert Juet, who kept a *Journal* in which he recorded his impressions of his introduction to the Indians. Although he felt the Indians could not be trusted, generally he found them friendly and hospitable and not well acquainted with the effects of alcohol. When a group of Indians was invited on board the *Half*

Moon and offered alcoholic refreshment, one became drunk and the others were confused, as alcohol "was strange to them."

Unfortunately, the Indian soon learned to crave alcohol and invariably drank himself into a state of total inebriation and moral abandonment. Brandy, wine and rum produced the same result. Since the Indian had no hereditary experience with fermented alcohol and since the high sugar content of his blood aided the process, a very few drinks reduced him into a staggering imbecile who suffered sad hallucinatory effects. As soon as one orgy wore off, he was ready to start another.

"There is," Father Le Jeune wrote in 1637, "scarcely a Savage, small or great, even among the girls and women, who does not enjoy this intoxication, and who does not take these beverages when they can be had, purely and simply for the sake of being drunk."

How the Lenni Lenape rose above this evil must be considered his greatest accomplishment. Over succeeding centuries, especially in seeking the northwestern fur trade, the French, British and Dutch were cruelly unscrupulous in playing upon Indian weaknesses. A new device, called "whiskey blanc" or "trader's rum" and "high wines," was used with cunning. For Indians unaccustomed to alcohol, a drink of one part of spirits to thirty-six of water was served, but as the habit quickened the proportions were reduced: to one part of spirits to six of water for hardened drinkers to a mixture of four to one for alcoholics. Horrible results followed. Under hallucinatory impulses the Indians raced around, sometimes calling out the names of demons who belonged to the legends of primitive religions. For no apparent motivation brother shot brother, husband slashed the throat of his wife, father threw children into fires.*

But the Lenni Lenape was a man who found within him-

* Walter D. Edmonds, *The Musket and the Cross* (Boston and Toronto, 1968), pp. 48–49.

self depths of emotional strength. His name could be trans-
lated into "Real Men," "Manly Men," "Original People"
and "Pure Indian," and his characteristics justified each
term. Among the Algonquins the Lenni Lenape were celebrated as the "Grandfathers" because of their political
leadership. The English placed them with the Delawares,
and the French called them *Loups*, or "Wolves."

Mystery surrounded their arrival in New Jersey. Apparently they had come from the Far West—that wild and
mountainous country where in time the Indians paid so
dearly for their attachment to "Trader's Rum." Centuries
before the trapper and his alcohol reached this western territory, the Lenni Lenape had migrated to the Mississippi,
where they lived among the Mengwe, or Iroquois. Here the
air vibrated with scouting reports of rich farm lands to the
east held by the Allegewi or Tallegewi (later the Chero-
kees).

The older men sat around council fires, smoking their
pipes and nodding as each spoke in turn. The flames fell on
the sober countenances of those who made the final decision:
let the war drums sound. Together Lenni Lenape and the
Iroquois seized tomahawks, spears and bows and arrows
and started the grim trek eastward. For a long time the war
drums pounded and blood soiled the ground all the way
from the Mississippi to the north of Virginia. The Iroquois
settled the northern half of this vast territory and the Lenni
Lenape the southern. With the suddenness of action that so
often startled other races, the friends became foes.

Master Feller spoke with a pride that matched the dig-
nity of the Lenni Lenape. They lived in wigwams and
"drest" in animal skins. The men were the hunters,
trappers, the fishermen, the warriors whereas the
women tended the crops. They made whatever they
needed: wooden and earthen dishes, axes from stone,

mats, hats and baskets from wild hemp roots and splints. They traveled in single file—the men in front, armed and watchful, and the women behind loaded with all the paraphernalia their backs could carry. They counted by tens and, when a number was too large for them to comprehend, they pointed to the stars or to the hairs of their heads.

There was very little sentimentality in Miss Fillips, and she described the manner of a Lenni Lenape wedding as what it was: an affair of intense domestic seriousness. About the age of eighteen a young man, ready to assume his full responsibilities, announced the name of the eligible maid— or the one among those "marriageable" girls wearing a red band around their foreheads—whom he wished to wed. All the members of the groom's clan assembled to discuss this prospective match. An extremely old man, clacking his tongue against toothless gums and sitting cross-legged like a tailor, praised the prospective bride for her prettiness. But those of a more practical turn of mind examined the girl's qualifications more penetratingly.

The atmosphere of the wigwam grew heated with the quickening discussion. How well had this maid been taught the crafts of her tribe? How adept was she in the arts of weaving, making wampum, cultivating the fields, or providing "the Indian life" poeticized by William Wood in his *New England Prospect*, 1639 edition:

> The dainty Indian maise
> Was eat with clamp-shells out of wooden trays,
> The luscious lobster with the craw-fish raw,
> The brinnish oyster, mussel, periwigge,
> And tortoise sought by the Indian squaw,
> Which to the flats danced many a winter's jigge,
> To dive for cockles and to dig for clams,
> Whereby her lazy husband's guts she cramms.

They spoke slowly, musically, these people who would add to our language such words as hickory and hominy, moccasin and moose, squash and succotash, quahog and woodchuck. The same melody was in their place names: Manahawkin, Absecon or Absequan and Abesegami, Tuckahoe, Manasquan, Rancocas, Hopatcong, Neshanic, Squankum, Mantoloking. They spoke in poetical images, relating themselves to events: the rising and the setting of the sun, the quartering of the moon, the awakening of spring, the coming of frost.

Before their eyes the proposed bride took shape as a working person. How well could she pucker the toes of a pair of moccasins? Or quillwork a deerskin belt? Or fashion the leggings that should be part of her own wedding dress? Hours passed as all opinions were fully explored.

"A good bride," commented the elder who had clucked his toothless gums over the maid's fine appearance. Then they turned to discussing the presents that should be offered the future wife as proof of approval of the groom's clan for the proposed wedding. Gifts of skins, fur and shell beads were added by various relatives until an impressive pile was assembled. Now a person unrelated to either clan but friendly to both was appointed to carry these presents to the wigwam of the girl.

So another family group assembled, this time to examine the good and bad points of the groom, whom most remembered since his babyhood. His physical appearance was evaluated. Was there a bright, firm tone to his tan skin? * Were his eyes large and set fairly apart, his nose straight, his lips strong but thin, his chin square and determined, his body tall and impressive, his muscles well developed?— characteristics that one male Lenni Lenape admired in another. How accurate was he with the bow, spear or, after

* The term "redskin" for an Indian was purely imaginative.

the white trader arrived, with a musket, and what other skills had he that reflected his ability as a hunter and provider and possible warrior in defense of an endangered tribe? The point was of great significance to the twelve hundred warriors of the two "Raritan Kings" who occupied the Scheyechbi (pronounced Shay-ak-bee), meaning "Long Land Water" (i.e., New Jersey), that stretched from the Hudson River to "Little Egg-bay and Sandy Barnegat." It was important also that the young man be skilled in fishing and gathering the shells used for trading. Was he adept in finding the periwinkles, conches and whelks that were converted into wampum or white money? Or the doubly valuable suckauhock, or black money, that could be made from clam shells? Or the beautiful two-sided necklaces of black and mother-of-pearl made from the shells of the mussel? *

When at last the young man was approved as a husband for the maid, the gifts of his clan were accepted and a day set for the wedding. And what an occasion that was! The groom was carefully attired, his hair slicked down with bear grease and his face patiently painted by his father. In festive garments the bride followed a procession to the Big House where the simple ceremonies were to be performed by the Chief and the Medicine Man. To Master Feller, Class of 1909, Stelton Grammar School, the grand moment of the marriage was when the groom presented the bride with a bone and received in return an ear of corn—symbolizing that during their lifetime he would supply the meat and she

* With great skill this money was polished, drilled with flints and strung into necklaces or belts. A string of 120 white beads was valued at a guilder by the Dutch and six pence by the English. A wampum belt of from twelve to eighteen rows of 180 beads was worth at least five shillings and probably more. Charles Edgar Nash, *The Lure of Long Beach* (Long Beach, N.J., 1936), p. 10. New Jersey's last wampum factory, operated to supply traders in the far west, existed along the banks of the Hackensack River near New Milford in the mid-19th century. James and Margaret Cawley, *Exploring the Little Rivers of New Jersey* (New Brunswick, N.J., 1961), p. 104.

the bread, as with wifely duty "her lazy husband's guts she cramms."

How long before the appearance of the white man the Indians of the Delaware wandered across New Jersey can only be conjectured. The best evidence we have measured by Carbon 14 tests of bone fragments dates their presence here at 1720 B.C., but samples of stone tools found in the Musconetcong Valley suggest that these descendants of Asiatic people may have preceded the white man by anywhere from four to ten thousand years. Before the offshore islands arose to form what is now Little Egg Harbor, the Indians who came before the Lenni Lenape insured their safety by building their homes on piles like Swiss lake dwellers.* Thus with their villages standing a quarter of a mile or farther from shore they lived in relative peace over many centuries. But in time evolution completed the creation of the offshore islands. The level of the bay waters changed, silt and muck under the pilings joined the villages to the mainland and covered over the huge mounds of clam and oyster shells. Thus the Lenni Lenape—or so the romance of history passed from father to son suggests—were able to attack them. One burial mound yields evidence of the ruthless slaying of men, women and children. The skeleton of one infant wore an amulet about its neck.

In the "Walam Olum" or "red painted sticks," where in symbols and pictographs the oral history of the eastern migration of the Lenni Lenape is preserved, occurs the legend of the Yah-qua-whee, or mastodon, a tale belonging to times almost forgotten. In this age the Great Spirit still appeared among his people and counseled them on how they must behave if they were to reach the happy hunting-ground.

The Yah-qua-whee, the Indians believed, had been placed

---

* Columbus found Indians on the coast of Venezuela who built their villages in a similar manner.

on earth to serve them as a beast of burden. But the mastodon, fierce in the knowledge of its own power, with a skin that could not be pierced by the sharpest spears or arrows, turned on all other creatures of the woods. Somewhere in the Ohio Valley, west of the Alleghenies, the final conflict raged, watched by the Great Spirit, who sat on a rock on a mountaintop.

Hordes of mastodons lumbered into battle. They swept away the mighty bear as though it were an insect. The slaughter became unbelievable as the mastodons struck with their snapping jaws and whipped their thorny tails. Blood streamed into the valleys. Soon the field of struggle became a reddened mire in which the very weight of the mastodons sank them in death.

The anger of the Great Spirit grew awesome. He stood upon the mountaintop, hurling bolts of lightning at the mastodons. One by one he killed all but an old bull, whose defiant tusks knocked aside the lightning bolts. In its rage, killing all who approached it, the old bull fought with a splendid, silent heroism. At last wounded, the bull dragged itself from the bloody mire. It bounded across the Ohio River, or so legend insists, and then across the Mississippi. It swam the Great Lakes and disappeared into the far north where it "lives to this day." *

Any who disbelieve this account of the mighty battle have only to search in the marshes and mires for the bones of the mastodons who expired. And there they will discover the cranberry, its coat colored in memory of the blood that flowed when the will of the Great Spirit prevailed. The legend of the Yah-qua-whee, which the Lenni Lenape brought with them when they settled Jersey soil, has been reinforced by some forty evidences of the presence of the mastodon or

* C. A. Weslager, *The Delaware Indians* (New Brunswick, N.J., 1972), pp. 92–93.

other "elephant-like" creatures that lived between the Hudson and Delaware rivers.

Great travelers by nature, with the coming of warm weather the inland Lenapes followed trails and rivers to live in the coolness of the Jersey seacoast. From long distances one could identify their presence for they paddled their canoes facing forward, which was exactly opposite the method of the white man, who propelled his small craft by rowing with his back to the prow.

For the Lenni Lenape happy days passed in their visit to the ocean shores of Scheyechbi and the offshore islands of the "Long Land Water." They fished and bathed in the waves, made wampum, and dozed in the high grass of sand dunes. Their toes curled in the lacework of the waves that covered their feet with sand. Many of the birds they knew —the yellow-crowned night heron, the harlequin duck, the king rail, the yellow rail, the black rail, the eastern bluebird, the prothonotary warbler, boat-tailed grackle and Henslow's sparrow—have grown so rare that they may have disappeared altogether; and so, too, have fish like the Atlantic sturgeon and red drum, amphibians and reptiles like the Eastern tiger salamander, the barking tree frog and eastern spiny softshell, or mammals like the southern hog lemming and harbor seal.

These were lazy days, but only in part. Shells for making wampum were industriously collected. Temporary wigwams of skins, bark and red cedar arose along the beaches. Old friendships with Indians who lived here the year round were renewed. Wampum and treaty belts accumulated. And briny breezes carried the squalls of newly born infants.

The visitors from inland forests gathered seaweed which, leached of its salt, enriched the soil it was plowed under. The king crabs which came ashore by the thousands to spawn in May and June were broken up and plowed under also. Only a few Indians lived the year through on the coast and offshore islands, and with the approach of winter storms they reinforced the bark of their wigwams and the grassy dunes that protected them from angry tempests. Autumn neared and inland dwellers began their trek homeward. Those who remained by the seashore filled their larders with geese and ducks.

The Lenni Lenape lived in peace and harmony with the white settlers. In 1758 near Atsion, in Burlington County, the Colonial Legislature purchased 3,044 acres for the exclusive use of the Indians, thus claiming to have established the first Indian reservation in America (called Edgepelick or Edgepillock, then Brotherton and now Indian Mills). Later the Indians sold their land in New Jersey, moved to the reservation of the Mohegans at Oneida Lake, New York, then to Green Bay, Wisconsin, and ultimately to the far western territory where they had originated. A warrior, Wilted Grass, who fought through the Revolution beside his white friends, also found a sympathetic response from the New Jersey Legislature when he insisted that his tribesmen never had been paid for their hunting and fishing rights. The members of the Legislature agreed and appropriated $2,000 to discharge this obligation. Wilted Grass replied with a letter of deep feeling:

"Not a drop of our blood have you spilled in battle; not an acre of our land have you taken but by our consent. These facts speak for themselves and need no comment. They place the character of New Jersey in bold relief, a bright example of those states within whose territorial limits our brethren still remain. Nothing save benisons can fall upon her from the lips of a Lenni-Lenape."

2

Lust in Rust

*Mefford R. Runyon—one of the six descendants of
the original French Huguenot settler, Vincent Runyon,
among the narrators for the Class of 1909—wore a
navy blue sash with British Union Jack and the date
1669 in white, representing the "British period." He
explained how the land had been bought from the Indians since Benajah Dunham had become the first settler of Piscataway, and his son Edmund, born in 1661,
was reputedly the first white baby to grow up playing
along the banks of the brooks feeding the Raritan
River. Master Runyon liked to go through history
with a hop, skip and jump. The liberal government
of the English, he declared, had made New Jersey
"worthy the name of Paradise" because in addition to
its natural advantages it had "no lawyers, or physicians, or parsons."*

In unison in all twenty-one counties of the State the descendants of the original Dutch settlers turned over in their
graves. If Master Runyon had wished a lesson in history,
he could have learned that almost two decades before Benajah Dunham settled in Piscataway stubborn Dutchmen had
explored "inland near the Raretang" for evidence of the
mineral wealth Indians said existed there. Moreover, among
Dutch settlers along the Delaware, in 1659 Claes de Ruyter
had found authentic specimens of copper and talked ex-

20

citedly of a crystal mountain containing gold. One would have thought that upon this proof the Dutch could have rolled back and rested in their graves, but these stubborn people never relinquished anything graciously, including a niggardly land policy, inept leadership or individual freedom in government—the three reasons why they failed to become successful colonizers in the New World.

Henry Hudson was gloomy and worried and his small crew verged on mutiny when he had his final glimpse of Sandy Hook. He had followed the river that now honors his memory as far as present-day Albany before he had realized that this waterway was not a fjord or strait leading to the fabled "northwest passage." Hudson carried home so much bad news that he convinced his sponsors of the Dutch East India Company to cross out the New World on their slate of future commercial opportunities.

But other Dutch speculators, organizing the United Netherland Company, dispatched new explorers to search for information Hudson could have missed. These men, coming unexpectedly out of the mists of the Atlantic, included Adriaen Block, mariner for merchants of Amsterdam and Hoorn, who with his fleet of five ships discovered "Hellegat" or Hellgate, the Housatonic and Connecticut rivers, Rhode Island and Block Island. When he had ascended the Hudson almost to Albany, his own vessel burned by accident. He pluckily built a new ship, the *Onrust,* a yacht forty-four and one-half feet long, in which he completed his explorations. The detailed "Figurative Map" of the southern New England coast, published in 1616 from data supplied by Block, became the basis of trading privileges in "New Netherland."

Whether Block ever returned to these scenes of New World adventure is unknown—very likely he did not, devoting the remainder of his life to commanding a whaling fleet near Spitzbergen. However, he was responsible for encouraging the organization of the Dutch West India Company, chartered in 1621, with colonization and trade within the areas Block had visited as its objectives. No government initiative ever aroused any activity of this sort in old Netherlands; such ventures were strictly "business affairs" and the governor or deputy general had to approve whatever action was taken.

Two classes of settlers existed: the "free," who received transportation and maintenance for the first two years and could own their own farms or bouweries, and "bound" farmers, required to work for stated terms on company lands, after which, not as Amsterdam, Rotterdam or Potterdam Dutch but as "the other dam Dutch," they were free to scratch for a living wherever they could find it. A kind of "melting pot" community grew out of this enterprise, including French-speaking Walloons, Flemings, Frenchmen, Germans and Englishmen. They settled on Governor's Island in the Upper Bay or in New York along the East River, or on the Delaware, or at Fort Nassau (later Fort Orange, now Albany).

The directors general of the West India Company were, in the gentlest of terms, a mixed lot. Peter Minuit, the Rhinelander, who in 1626 dangled trinkets to the value of sixty guilders (about twenty-four dollars) before a group of Indian chiefs and purchased Manhattan Island, was vain and brilliant and extremely adept at placing his self-interest before the public welfare. He never refused to quarrel with anyone, including his sponsors, and all were soon glad to part company, whereupon the wily Minuit planned the establishment of a Swedish colony in the New World. As Minuit's successor, Wouter Van Twiller, a youthful desk clerk, was never expected to be more than an interim appointment, and hostile officials made certain that this anticipation was fulfilled. In 1637 William Kieft, an Amsterdam merchant, succeeded the desk clerk. Kieft could keep the patroons in their place, but only until the Indians became involved, whom he treated with an arrogant ignorance and produced a fearful massacre.

In 1630 the first Dutchman to cross the Hudson into New Jersey was Michael Pauw. He was given a large tract of land, called "Hobocan" by the Indians, and an adjoining tract that he named Pavonia. Pauw claimed none of the gifts required of a successful colonist. He never attracted the minimum number of settlers to justify holding these tracts. A house was built at Communipaw in 1633 and another at Pavonia a few years later. Pauw finally was recalled by the Dutch West India Company, and thereafter Dutch settlers multiplied along the west bank of the Hudson.

The Indian remained an obstacle to the Dutch style of tight-fisted colonizing. Since archeologists have located almost two thousand aboriginal sites, the Indians must have seemed to the colonists to exist everywhere, and their travels over three well-established trails must have added to this illusion.* In 1643 traders at Rensselaerwyck and Fort Orange persuaded the Mohawks to attack the Indians on the lower Hudson, after which the Mohawks were to seek refuge among the Dutch of Manhattan and Jersey. Kieft completely misread the situation. He led a savage and devastating assault upon the friendly Mohawks. Indian reprisals followed quickly, including the destruction of Pavonia.

Kieft by now was thoroughly hated by the Indians and the Dutch. Settlers south of Albany fled to a wall built across Manhattan Island. And in 1646 Kieft was replaced

* The Minisink path led from the upper Delaware to Matawan and the shore; the Burlington Trail connected that community on the Delaware with Cape May; and the Manahawkin Trail ran from Camden to Tuckerton. In addition numerous minor paths were used. Richard P. McCormick, *New Jersey from Colony to State, 1609–1789* (New Brunswick, N.J., 1964), p. 8.

by that most colorful of all Dutch directors general—
tenacious Peter Stuyvesant with his wooden leg.

A decade passed peaceably and Dutch farms dotted the
landscape between Hoboken and Bayonne. Then in September, 1655, Stuyvesant led an expedition against the Swedes
on the lower Delaware. The Indians struck anew with the
tomahawk and fire arrow, and muskets bartered from
Dutch traders in Connecticut. Once more Pavonia became a
waste of ashes. The Dutch fled across the Hudson and
could not be persuaded to resettle in New Jersey until 1660,
when the town of Bergen rose on the heights beyond Communipaw. Town plots were awarded the settlers, their own
courts established, and a shadowy form of self-government
was adopted. In fifty years the Dutch had established only
two small villages. Almost everything was a question of
too little and too late with the Dutch West India Company.

The final crisis came in August of 1664, when a task
force of four British frigates sailed into New York Bay.
Old Peter Stuyvesant pounded his wooden peg and thrust
two large pistols in his belt. With cajolery, then anger, he
pleaded for a stalwart defense. His council shuddered at
the prospect of bloodshed and, we are told, left the meeting
"dodging through narrow lanes and alleys, starting at every
little dog that barked, mistaking lamp posts for British
grenadiers."

Stuyvesant shouted until veins bulged in his forehead. He
flashed his pair of pistols. The Dutch nailed up their doors
and awaited their inevitable conquest by the British, surrendering "without a blow or a tear."

At this point Master Runyon caught up with the main-
stream of history. In that year of defeat for the Dutch
the Duke of York received other land tracts from his
brother, King Charles II. He was satisfied to divide
the colony into East and West Jersey and explained

*how the land lying between the Hudson and Delaware
rivers had been called New Jersey in honor of Sir
George Carteret, a former governor of the "iland"
of Jersey.*

Untangling New Jersey's colonial history, especially after
the arrival of the English, is like wandering through a
maze. The first King Charles included New Jersey in the
vaguely defined empire he gave to Sir Edmund Plowden
(1634). Calling this territory New Albion (and himself
Earl Palatine), the proprietor dreamed of restoring the
age when knighthood was in flower. He talked of twenty-
three Indian kings whom he expected to convert, again an
invention of his imagination. Meanwhile about sixty New
Englanders, weary of the excessive discipline of the New
Haven Colony, settled at Salem on the Delaware but were
repeatedly chased away by the Swedes.

In 1660 Charles II ascended the throne as poor as a
royal church mouse could get. He paid off his creditors as
best he could and was particularly generous to his brother,
James, the Duke of York, who created East Jersey and
West Jersey. However, Colonel Richard Nicolls, whom
the Duke made governor, already was causing future prob-
lems by permitting a group of settlers from Jamaica, Long
Island, to purchase from the Indians land between the Raritan and Passaic rivers for twenty fathoms of trading cloth,
two coats, two guns, two kettles, ten bars of lead, twenty
handfuls of powder, and four hundred fathoms of white
wampum. The "Monmouth Grant"—a vague area, about a
dozen miles wide and bounded by Sandy Hook and the
south side of Raritan Bay—was established on a seven-year
rent-free basis by Baptists from Rhode Island and Quakers
from Gravesend, Long Island (the original Quaker Meet-
inghouse in Shrewsbury still stands).

Sir George Carteret decided to live with circumstances

as they existed in East Jersey. He sent his cousin, Philip Carteret, to govern the proprietorship from its first capital of Elizabethtown, presumably so named in honor of Sir George's wife. A "Frame of Government," liberal for its time in correcting court abuses and condoning religious freedom, was adopted. Robert Treat brought his disenchanted New Englanders from the New Haven Colony to settle in Newark. New England Baptists from Piscataqua, the name of an Indian tribe in Maine and also of a river that divided Maine and New Hampshire, settled Piscataway. The Dutch pushed inland to the Hackensack and Passaic rivers.

But the muddle of the Jerseys was just beginning. The two parts were united into one royal colony and then once more separated. The situation must have caused John Lord Berkeley considerable embarrassment, for he already had sold his interest in West Jersey for a thousand pounds to John Fenwick and Edward Byllynge, influential Quakers. For a time William Penn was involved in the negotiations before discovering that the settlement of Pennsylvania was all he could handle. Understandably, some land titles could not be untangled in less than a century.

The most fascinating villain among the royal governors was Edward Hyde Cornbury, a viscount, first cousin to Queen Anne and the black sheep of an otherwise notable family. Cornbury was a transvestite and enjoyed the clothes and behavior of the opposite sex. Startled visitors stammered out their affairs to the governor wearing a dress, and if midway through such discussions Cornbury asked to be excused and reappeared in masculine attire, the visitor had received the cruellest of royal snubs. Official functions found Cornbury extravagantly begowned, bejeweled and bewigged. If a lady attended in similar costume, Cornbury stalked off in a rage. Later he would return in a more dazzling gown, for he always insisted on believing that he was the belle of the ball. During his administration in the early eighteenth century he fought with everyone—over religion, quitrents, taxes, elections.

If Miss Fillips knew the meaning of "transvestite," she certainly was not sharing that information with the members of the Class of 1909, nor was she discussing piracy, which had prospered along the seacoast since early colonial times. America's first true novelist, James Fenimore Cooper, who was born in Burlington, did not require historical context to connect Lord Cornbury to that prince of Atlantic Ocean pirates, Captain William Kidd.

Modern New Jerseymen who look down from the Highlands upon Sandy Hook probably do not realize that those sandy beaches are a geological marvel, fashioned grain by grain by the sands of the Navesink and Shrewsbury rivers. Whales once washed ashore in nearby Spermaceti Cove. The Twin Lights of the Highlands, originally intended to guide ships into the Navesink and Shrewsbury, are now a museum.

Cooper gave Raritan Bay lasting fame when he made the area around Sandy Hook the locale for his novel, *The Water-Witch,* in which one of his principal characters, the Skimmer, was inspired by the legends of Captain William Kidd. Although the book is set in the 1720s and the real Captain Kidd died before Lord Cornbury became the first royal governor of New Jersey (1702–1708), in Cooper's book they are contemporaries.

In 1697, at the time Kidd was sailing the seas as a privateer, Jeremiah Basse was appointed governor of East and West Jersey by the proprietors. In order to gain royal favor, Basse took action against the pirates who sought refuge on the Jersey shore, and he attempted to show that the Scottish proprietors at Perth Amboy were working with the pirates. But his rule caused so much dissension among the proprietors that he was removed from office in 1699. When Lord Cornbury became governor, Basse was appointed secretary and so was included in the ill fame of that corrupt government.

Sympathetic biographers of the real Lord Cornbury could excuse his odd behavior on the grounds that as a cousin of Queen Anne he long had wished to imitate this illustrious kinswoman, but Queen Anne was scarcely an excuse for Cornbury's growing reputation in life as "a spendthrift, a 'grafter,' a bigoted oppressor and a drunken, vain fool." Never, said one Tory biographer, had the colony possessed "a governor so universally detested."

Kidd had been commissioned December 11, 1695, as captain of a private man-of-war to attack and capture enemy ships (French) and pirate ships, with the agreement that, if he did not take any prizes, neither he nor his crew would be paid. He sailed from Plymouth on April 23, 1696, in the *Adventure Galley,* and upon reaching New York he completed his crew. According to official documents, "many flockt to him from all parts, men of desperate fortunes and necessitous in expectation of getting vast treasures. . . . 'twill not be in Kidd's power to govern such a hord of men under no pay."

After nearly a year without earning a penny, Kidd's crew threatened mutiny. "The Dying Words of *Capt.* Robert [William] Kidd," published in Providence late in the eighteenth century and still available in collections of American folklore, related the awesome result when William Kidd, a man of unreasonable temper, struck a bucket upon the head of William Moore, one of his gunners:

> I'd a bible in my hand, when I sail'd, when I sail'd,
>   I'd a bible in my hand when I sail'd,
> I'd a bible in my hand by my father's great command,
>   But I sunk it in the sand when I sail'd.

I murder'd William Moore, as I sail'd, as I sail'd,
    I murder'd William Moore as I sail'd;
I murder'd William Moore, and I left him in his gore,
    Not many leagues from shore, as I sail'd.

Kidd, destined now to be hanged as Moore's murderer, could not see where he had anything to lose by turning pirate. Legends spread of the fortunes he secured. One of the richest, rumor said, was buried beside a pine tree on Sandy Hook. One of Kidd's most distinguished biographers * gives full credence to the rumor of fortunes amassed by Kidd: ". . . Governor Basse of New Jersey had taken from Kidd's men thousands of pieces of eight, Rix dollars, and Venetians, not to say anything of Arabian gold, amber and coral necklaces, and India silks."

Tricked by the promise of a pardon into landing in Boston, Kidd and his men were captured and sent to England. When questioned by the House of Commons, Kidd would not disclose the names of the English noblemen who had underwritten many of his ventures. On May 8, 1701, he was tried for the murder of his gunner and for piracy, found guilty and on May 9 sentenced to be hanged:

To Execution Dock, I must go, I must go,
    To Execution Dock, I must go;
To Execution Dock, where many thousands flock,
    But I must bear my shock, and must die.

Come all ye young and old, see me die, see me die,
    Come all ye young and old, see me die;
Come all ye young and old, you're welcome to my gold,
    For by it I've lost my soul, and must die.

James Fenimore Cooper, the first American author to win international acclaim— for such Leather Stocking novels

* Willard Hallam Bonner, *Pirate Laureate: The Life and Legends of Captain Kidd* (New Brunswick, N.J., 1947), p. 116.

as *The Pioneers* and *The Last of the Mohicans,* for his invincible hero Natty Bumppo, and such unforgettable characters as Uncas and Chingachgook—was always drawn to stories of the sea. Cooper was engaged in collecting material for a naval history when the tales of Kidd and Lord Cornbury seized his imagination. For three months through a Paris winter Cooper worked day and night to create a legend he called *The Water-Witch.* Cooper considered the work among his poorest; it may have been his best.

Highlands, New Jersey, looks down on Sandy Hook and the rumored abode of the half-phantom outlaw, "The Skimmer of the Seas," who is Kidd in Cooper's novel. The Skimmer's patroness, the Water-Witch, whose figurehead adorns his sleek, black brigantine, gives her name to his magical craft. Cooper draws upon many fantasies, including that of *The Flying Dutchman,* to tell about the Skimmer's illicit trade with supposedly respectable Jersey men. To the question, "And pray friend who is this Skimmer of the Seas?" an apparently informed source yields a bewildering reply:

"The witches may tell! I only know that such a rover there is, and that he is here today and there tomorrow. Some say that it is only a craft of mist that skims the top of the seas . . . and others think it is the sprite of a vessel that was rifled and burnt by Kidd in the Indian Ocean, looking for its gold and the killed."

Strange rites, presided over by the Water-Witch, were observed aboard the Skimmer's brigantine—rites to chill the blood of those who believed the once terrifying tales of witchcraft in New England. Principal events in *The Water-Witch* are dominated by the Skimmer and a highly respected Dutch "mynheer," Alderman Van Beverout, whose summer mansion on the west bank of the Shrewsbury River bore the intriguing name of "Lust in Rust." In an argument with Euclid, his colored servant, Van Beverout characterizes

Kidd as "a rank rogue;" and as many of Kidd's crew were
dark-skinned, the Dutchman adds: "His fate should be a
warning to every nigger in the colony." Euclid haughtily
refused to be classed with Kidd's blacks, who were "Guinea-
born."

Cornbury warns the burgher that "the second part of
the tragedy of Kidd may yet be enacted in these seas."
Van Beverout shrugs and answers almost impudently: "I
leave such enterprise to my superiors. . . . Enterprises
that are said to have occupied the Earl of Bellomont,
Governor Fletcher, and my Lord Cornbury, are above the
ambitions of an humble merchant."

From the balcony of her bedroom at Lust in Rust the
Dutchman's niece, Alida, scanning the bay, observes the
Water-Witch sailing into a nearby hidden cove, where it
anchors. For what purpose, if not to plunder the mansion?
But when the Skimmer arrives at the mansion, he and Van
Beverout transact their affairs in a jovial mood.

Alida's suitor, Captain Cornelius Van Cuyler Ludlow of
Her Majesty's cruiser *Coquette,* determines to capture the
Skimmer. The chase is desperate. The *Water-Witch* plunges
through Hell Gate into Long Island Sound followed by the
Coquette. The latter is deflected from the chase by an in-
decisive battle with a French vessel. The Skimmer suddenly
appears on board Ludlow's ship to warn him of another im-
minent attack by the French, and then disappears. When the
Frenchmen board the *Coquette* in overwhelming numbers,
he reappears to fight on the British side. Then the ship
bursts into flames. Ludlow, Alida, the Skimmer, and others
escape on a hastily constructed raft and are finally rescued
by the *Water-Witch.*

The Skimmer, after putting his guests safely ashore, sails
off, vowing never to haunt these coasts again. The Skimmer
was far too romanticized to represent the true Kidd; to
Cooper he was an American Robin Hood, filled with the

spirit of independence that defied the law and won freedom from the British.

Captain Kidd may have been more intimately associated with Monmouth County than many readers (including the author) of *Water-Witch* suspected. The tomb of William Leeds, believed to have been one of Kidd's chief lieutenants, is in the Christ Episcopal Church cemetery at Shrewsbury. Originally the inscription was on lead, which patriots melted down to make bullets during the Revolutionary War. A bronze plaque has been substituted.

3

The Morristown Mob

Master Arthur D. Drake described the area after eighty years. Piscataway now contained 40,000 acres and some eighty families numbering more than four hundred persons. Two or three men could clear fifty or sixty acres in a year and houses were constructed from the trees. Stones picked from the fields or bricks imported from England supplied chimneys until the settlers discovered that the clay around Amboy made excellent bricks. Iron nails cost more than the remainder of the house, and none but the very rich could afford glass windows. Open fireplaces provided the means for cooking, and brick ovens set in the chimney walls baked bread, cake, pies and puddings. The Town House, opened in 1682, contained the county court (which also met in Woodbridge and Amboy). The Colonial Legislature met at least once (1679) in Piscatawaytown; every Sunday religious services were held in the Town House; here "all public matters were discust and decided"; and here "criminals were condemd to the stock or whipping post." In 1689 the first Baptist Church was founded with six members, "the second oldest Baptist church in New Jersey, and either the tenth or twelfth oldest in the United States."

The rousing stories of New Jersey at this time Master Drake had not heard. They concerned pirates who coasted

33

beneath the black flag along the Jersey beaches and counterfeiters who frequented New Jersey's inland swamps and
mountains.

The Dutch, English and French were equally guilty of
bringing piracy to the New World, and if any one of this
trio attempted to look demurely innocent upon raising this
subject he should have had a spike with a Jolly Roger driven
into his cranium. The more than one hundred miles of Jersey seacoast were bound to attract its share of brigands, if
only to seek refuge in times of storm. Some, certainly, may
have arrived looking for a cache for their "ill-gotten loot."
Among the first to do so was the Dutch vessel *Holy Ghost,*
"burthen about 160 tuns" and bearing a "great treasury"
when she cleared Amsterdam. In 1653 the crew of the *Holy
Ghost* joined a "wild band" in the harbor of Barbados.
Fifty miles from Boston the *Holy Ghost* was overtaken by
a British trading ship and towed into the Massachusetts
port, but captain and crew were ultimately released for want
of evidence—with "profit for all"—when they sailed from
Boston to New Jersey. Rumor has long declared that they
buried their treasure on one of the offshore islands.

The unhappy end of Captain William Kidd was entirely
unpredictable. When he left England in 1696 in the *Adventure Galley,* his mission was to clear the seas of pirates. But,
as we have learned, his temper leading to the murder of
Moore, the gunner, caused his undoing. Thereafter, his experiences as a pirate, first aboard the *Quedagh Merchant,*
an Armenian ship, and then the *Antonio,* a Yankee sloop,
ended in May, 1701. Ten men, their bodies tarred, hanged
with him from a gibbet on the shores of the Thames.

So when the chant broke out—

> Yo ho, the wind doth blow,
> Pirates on Barnegat Bay

—no one could be certain of the identity of the culprits. John Quelch, whose vandals preyed upon the Portuguese? Captain Charles Vane, whose cutthroats fattened on the silver of the Spaniards? Worley, with his unsavory crew of eight and six muskets, who darted out of New York Harbor to plunder any type of coastal shipping? The fierce Blackbeard with long sulphur matches stuck behind his hairy ears? Or one of Barnegat's own reputed crop of pirates?

Unknown to Master Drake was a tale, now almost a century old, related by the residents of Long Beach Island. One evening when the setting sun was blood red and a delight to the hearts of all sailors, a sloop dropped anchor about two hundred yards off shore. Presently two seamen in the knit caps that then were a mark of their calling rowed a yawl through the breakers to a safe landing. They were a pleasant, good-humored pair who quickly won the respect of the Coast Guard crew.

"Are there two cedars growing close together on this beach?" they asked.

"Aye," the superintendent replied. "Not far from where the old lighthouse stood."

"May we spend the evening here and explore the place more carefully in the morning?"

"Aye. An' we'll all help ye."

If the visitors minded this interference they gave no indication. They talked as sailors so often do—about the sea. Thus the couple learned that to the north of the island the bay was joined to the ocean by what the Dutch had named "Barendegat," meaning "Breaker's Inlet," or "Inlet of the Breakers."

"I've heard of eighty cod caught in that inlet in two hours," the superintendent said. "And better by far than any cod you can catch in New England."

The conversation passed pleasantly until one newcomer suggested that in view of all they wished to accomplish by daylight they should sleep early. The idea seemed generally appealing. With dawn the sun began to cast brilliant shafts of light above the horizon. The lookout in the tower of the Life Saving Station burst into a roar:

"They're gone!"

Through a spyglass he spotted the pair. Apparently they had spent the night digging a deep hole between the cedars. Now they hoisted aloft an iron-bound chest that obviously was too heavy for them to carry. They ripped open the chest and dumped its contents into bags that were far more manageable. Shouts rang above the breakers as the Coast Guard crew chased their late friends. Half dragging, half carrying their bags, the intruders won the race to the yawl. They laughed at their pursuers, lined up along the beach and shaking their fists.

A few Spanish coins scattered in the sand and a rusty cutlass were the only gifts they left their benefactors.

In the half-century my aging legs have shuffled this coast I have yet to uncover my first Spanish doubloon. Old-timers say buried treasure is more likely to be found in the northern than southern part of the State. I guess I have been trudging in the wrong direction.

Counterfeiters brought their craft to the New World aboard the *Mayflower,* and probably only the horse thief was more common among colonial criminals. At counterfeiting none outshone New Jersey's Samuel Ford, who was ultimately celebrated as "the most accomplished [forger] this country ever produced." The Ford family had settled in Monroe, two miles east of Morristown, where they received a gift of land in 1721. Samuel gave every appearance of respectability when he married Grace Kitchell of Hanover, the sister of a future United States Senator. They had four children.

Ford's reliability again was vouchsafed by the fact that

he worked with that noted Scotsman, William Alexander, Lord Stirling, in the iron works at Hibernia, but the mines consistently accumulated debts and faced bankruptcy. In order to save his own skin Benjamin Cooper, one of the miners, secretly suggested to Samuel that he practice the arts that would turn the place into a front for counterfeiting operations.

There was danger in this kind of makeshift enterprise, Samuel knew; he sold out his interest in the mine at Hibernia and journeyed to Ireland, apparently to improve his skill as a counterfeiter. Despite his previous marriage he wed an Irish girl and brought his new wife to America in 1766. Neither spouse wished to be called a bigamist (Ford's second wife, it was said, married an Irishman in Whippany, New Jersey), but Samuel took these matters lightly.

Ford now established his New Jersey operation at "Hammock," a farm of over one hundred acres at Hanover. What cheered Samuel about the place was an almost impenetrable swamp surrounding his proposed site of operations. He achieved the arts of engraving and type-making as though he had been born with these talents. The days were busy. Captain Joseph Richardson of Philadelphia supplied him with types. Besides Captain Richardson, he also enlisted in his illicit business John King, an undersheriff of Morris County, and, as Ford's business grew, the number of unsavory characters increased around Hanover. Generally they were known as the "Morristown Mob." *

Samuel Ford disliked a career in crime. It was, he believed, a dehumanizing, back-breaking occupation, ill paid for the risks involved. He was a good-looking man, huskily built, who should have been able to earn an honest living. Still, it was difficult to go straight when one of your cronies

* Kenneth Scott, *Counterfeiting in Colonial America* (New York, 1957), pp. 236ff.; also, "The Middlesex Counterfeiters," *Proceedings of the New Jersey Historical Society* (Newark, N.J., 1952), pp. 246–49.

was Thomas Kinney, high sheriff of Morris County. The culprits escaped prosecution—"for want of evidence."

At Hanover, Ford determined to specialize in forging Pennsylvania and New Jersey bills. All connected with the enterprise in any way were sworn to secrecy that an island in the swamp was the scene of operations. Ford left "Hammock" carrying a rifle so that if he were noticed by some other early riser he would be mistaken for a farmer off on a day's hunt. Although most of the swamp could be easily navigated through knee-deep water, the last few shallow yards had to be crawled on the stomach. How Ford hated this final part of the journey! Sometimes the floating muck-soaked tree branches felt like underwater snakes. And here he was, undoubtedly the best forger in the colonies, forced to slither on his belly for a living!

But Ford also enjoyed moments of exultation. His counterfeit paper approximated perfection. The types from which he struck off his three-pound and thirty-shilling Jersey and Pennsylvania bills were adjudged masterpieces of duplication. Even the studied scrutiny of State treasurers could not discover their small flaws, and Ford chuckled at his reputation of "treasurer for the three provinces." He forged the signatures on all his own notes.

Business expanded. An invaluable ally was John King, one-time undersheriff of Morris County. King was a pleasant fellow, about eight or nine inches above five feet so he could not attract too much attention. Short, brown, straight hair emphasized a full face. Captain Richardson of Philadelphia, another unfailing ally, was judged in September, 1773, to be about forty-three years of age, six feet in height, stout, active, fair of skin and "smooth of speech." Squire Moses Ayres, justice of the peace of Sussex County, was said to have a touch-and-go relationship with the Morristown Mob (but, apparently, more touch than go). Other "acquaintances" were described as "remarkably handsome men" and "descended from the first families" of Hanover.

Rewards were offered for prominently known associates of Ford's gang. Some accusations were made, but bungled by the members of the Provincial Council, so that none was brought to justice. Ford was arrested and jailed in July, 1773, but escaped with the help of John King. The governor was red-faced in his anger over these escapes and demanded that a Grand Jury be assembled.

Samuel Ford found the times propitious for evaporating into the swamp mists. The governor's men appeared everywhere, sniffing like bloodhounds for suspects. The few caught were freed by overnervous accomplices within the governor's "official" family. But time and hard sleuthing led to the revelation of the full plot; a number were arrested and a few sentenced to execution.

The hanging was held in Perth Amboy, capital of East Jersey. Wives and mothers, tears rolling down their cheeks, clung to the governor's coat-tails as they pleaded for the release of their husbands and sons. The governor stood his ground pitilessly; but only David Reynolds, a farmer, was hanged.

Various colonies offered rewards for Ford. They duelled with a will-o'-the-wisp. Soon it was reported that Ford had discovered another swamp, where he happily forged money for Maryland, Pennsylvania and New Jersey. He married for a third time and became a silversmith in what is now West Virginia.

4

His Noodle Meditating Song

The applause quickened when Miss Evelyn R. Letson, a descendant of the township's oldest settlers (Francis Drake, Vincent Runyon, Poincet Stelle), held the sides of her skirt and curtsied. Evelyn covered the early years of the Revolution. Coach lines now connected New York and Philadelphia. The journey in the big, clumsy, covered wagons required three days. Upon occasion, to say the least, the trip was scarcely a joy: "Often the farmers here were cald upon to go out with their oxen and pull the stage out of a mudhole . . . and sometimes they were askt to help take [the stage] on its way to Newark or New Brunswick." That thriving community now contained four streets, of which the most prominent was named Albany Street by the Dutch who had migrated from upstate New York. "Small yachts"—and "wooden vessels, too," products of the town's one shipbuilding yard—transformed the Raritan River into a busy thoroughfare for the shipment of corn, flour, "bred," linseed and timber.

Small businesses, instilling within their entrepreneurs a deepening spirit of self-dependence and rebellion toward arbitrary government, flourished throughout the colonies. But New Jersey added something more: the first American poet to win international acclaim. He was at his best writing in frontier idiom and wit and equally at ease whether describing a drunken parson or himself:

> His belly was not over-full,
> His jerkin would not bear a pull,
> Dejectedly he walk'd along,
> His noodle meditating song.

The Freneau (originally Fresneau) family were among the French Protestants who became wanderers from religious persecution following the revocation of the Edict of Nantes (1685). The Freneaus, luckier than many Huguenots, had prospered as importers of wine from France and the Canary Islands, but this good fortune did not follow them when they reached the New World in 1709. Here they encountered numerous discouragements, though they embraced any opportunity to outwit adversity. They farmed on Long Island. They were land speculators in New York. They invested in copper mining in Connecticut. They were importers and exporters with an office in Charleston, South Carolina, but their exchange of beeswax, codfish, nails, beans and Indian corn for Madeira wine was singularly unsuccessful.

Temporarily at least Pierre Freneau's fortunes appeared on the upswing when finally he turned to "agricultural pursuits" in New Jersey. In 1750 he married Agnes Watson and two years later moved from New York City with their infant son to a house he built on land owned by his wife's family in Monmouth County. Pierre was a man of cultivated tastes and an ardent admirer of fine paintings and books, attributes that his oldest son, Philip, inherited. Just one week after Philip's birth on January 2, 1752 (o.s.), the skies were ablaze with the blue and red lights of the aurora borealis. It was an omen, the country folk declared. The babe was certain to make his mark in history; and so Philip did, as "The Poet of the Revolution" and as the man, in Thomas Jefferson's judgment, who saved the government when it was "galloping fast into monarchy."

Philip's earliest years were passed at "Locust Grove" in Mount Pleasant (in Matawan Township), not more than two miles south from Middletown Point, a shipping center on Raritan Bay, where the shore of the bay turned toward Amboy. He lived among pleasant meadows and sandy fields protected from the ravages of summer or winter storms by the Navesink Highlands. During hot weather dust warmed his bare toes as he shuffled along the lane. Friendly garter snakes slithered by. He muttered a great deal to himself— this lad with "his noodle meditating song"—but his neighbors, old Scot, British and Dutch farmers named Holmes and Schenck and Van Pelt greeted him with cheery smiles and hand waves.

His mother, a good, intelligent woman, would comfort the child against her big bosom. She read to him from her own copy of the Book of Common Prayer and sometimes from *The Works of the Late Reverend Isaac Watts,* guaranteed to produce slumber within a quarter of an hour for any growing boy. He was drawn irresistibly to his father's collected works of Shakespeare. One of the lad's earliest examples of "noodling" appeared on the end papers of his father's copy of *The Spectator:*

> Dont steal this Book My Honest Friend
> For Fear the Gallows will be your end
> And then the Justis will come and say
> Where is the Book you Stole away
>   Philip Freneau

Mount Pleasant and nearby Middletown Point offered cheerful surroundings for a growing boy. Pine and juniper scented the surrounding countryside. Wild huckleberries grew almost everywhere. Coves of brooks and the bay always promised the excitement of discovering a pirate's treasure. A sawmill buzzed with activity as timbers were cut for local buildings and a tower of logs provided protection against the ravages of winter.

But when snow and ice limited the traffic of the round-bottomed boats at Middletown Point, what fun excelled a brisk race between horse-drawn sleighs? Whips cracked. Hand-wrought iron runners struck sparks when hard surfaces cropped through the snow. Sleigh bells jangled. Inevitably competing vehicles approached curves on even terms.

Tense, reddened faces peered from beneath woolen caps. Scarves flapped in the breeze. Under the snapping of the whips the horses strained until flecks of foam blew from their mouths. The sleighs touched, bounced aside, scraped sides anew. The inevitable could be predicted. One sleigh or both tipped over. The horses thrashed in the roadside snowbanks and the riders rolled across the field like furry balls.

Philip was an obedient, conscientious student, learning his first lessons at his mother's knee. He may have spent a year away at school in New York City, but the evidence is fuzzy. There is no doubt, however, that he attended Mattisonia Grammar School in Manalapan, some fifteen miles from Mount Pleasant. There Alexander Mitchell, a young graduate from Princeton, and the Reverend William Tennent, whose church stood on the edge of the fields where the Battle of Monmouth would be fought, prepared Philip for college. He read in Horace, Cicero, the Greek Testament, Lucian and Xenophon while mastering composition in English and Latin.

Pierre Freneau wished his oldest son to become a parson —a prospect that roiled like a bad oyster in Philip's stomach. The youth's sensitivity helped him to understand his father's growing unhappiness. Here was a man who had traveled to exotic ports, who spoke a dozen languages, who had slumbered under moons above and below the tropics. His family increased—babies arriving on schedule almost like stagecoaches—so that from year to year he was bound to a life that stretched no farther than from Mount Pleasant to Middletown Point. A second son died of smallpox, the great fear of the age, and Pierre shriveled more deeply within himself. He would never escape except through death —which occurred on October 17, 1767.

Philip understood; Philip sorrowed. On the last page of his father's letterbook he wrote: "Here ends a Book of Vexation."

Then, loyal son that he was, Philip set off to become a parson.

Sixteen-year-old Philip entered Princeton in 1768 as a sophomore, a compliment to the boy and his tutors. From miles away young Freneau could see the massive stone walls of Nassau Hall, a landmark modeled after King's College at Cambridge. That irresistible man of unflinching Presbyterian spirit, John Witherspoon, Princeton's new president, won friendly smiles by declaring that nothing at the University of Edinburgh equaled Princeton's beauty. Philip, who had ridden through forty miles of rolling meadows and forests to reach the college, was even awestruck by the country village of fifty or so houses surrounding the college. A row of buttonwood trees shielded the building from the dust and clatter of the main highway. Beyond young Philip gazed at a bust of Homer and then at four tiers of windows. The belfry looked out of place where so much symmetry abounded; it was like a high hat left forgotten on a hallway rack.

The fright of strangeness did not linger long with Philip or any of the approximately one hundred and fifty students who lived, ate and studied in Nassau Hall. John Wither-spoon, who as the spiritual leader of the college believed firmly that the devil found work for idle hands, made cer-tain Old Nick would find meager encouragement at Prince-ton. The college bell awakened the countryside at five in the morning. Sleepy-eyed students showered epithets upon crooked stocking seams, for tutors and Witherspoon appar-ently assumed that no truly upright person would attend chapel in unseemly apparel. Morning services were a serious affair, followed by a period of study until breakfast at eight.

Morning recitations began at nine. Until the midday meal Philip discoursed upon the classics, the "compleat" system of geography, the basic principles of philosophy and "the elements of mathematical knowledge." Ultimately Philip would add to this curriculum Dr. Witherspoon's lectures on moral philosophy, but the chore was far less onerous than most students expected. Witherspoon was an alert, smiling, profound, easy-going speaker in the classroom, whereas on public occasions he tended to reveal a nervousness by flash-ing his heavy eyebrows or continually shifting his hands and feet. Upon one patriotic affair, it was said, the good doctor was in the midst of an oration when a cannon was fired acci-dentally, whereupon Witherspoon "sprang forward as if in a convulsion." The president regained his composure with obvious difficulty, but he was always adaptable to human surprises, even when expounding upon the subject of scien-tific agriculture, of which he probably did not know half as much as he claimed.

"Doctor," one critic remarked, "I see no flowers in your garden."

"No, nor in my discourses either," Witherspoon retorted, probably regretting his sharpness afterward, for there was not a tinge of real meanness in the man.

Witherspoon's Princeton provided excellent academic soil for Philip Freneau's intellectual growth. True, his day

did not end until after various orations before the whole
student body in the main hall at five. Supper followed, usually at six, and the remainder of the day was his—that is,
until the college bell sounded curfew at nine. Quite clearly,
within limits, Witherspoon possessed that Scottish prudence
which could place out of mind what was not within sight.
There were then, as there are still, "fools" in the college
cast who spent their leisure in the village "eating, drinking,
dancing and fiddling . . . [and] playing [cards] for pennies." But once curfew rang, neither cajolery nor threat
could persuade Kelsey, the innkeeper, to sell another drop
of wine or rum. The man would react shiftily as though he
felt above his head the invisible presence of Witherspoon's
clenched fist.

Philip was not one of the crowd eager to exchange gown
for town. In fact, college for him was like a torrent of
books, a boiling, tempestuous outpouring of ideas, in which
he bounced and bobbled half-submerged, but always sur-
faced as lithesomely as a floating feather. The poet in
Philip was excited by the formations and images he discovered in Homer and Milton and Pope—indeed, so much so,
that half a literary lifetime passed before he rose above
imitating their examples and allowed his superb Americanism
to emerge.

To think of Philip as a studious little stuffed shirt is
neither accurate nor fair. The Boston Massacre, occurring
during Philip's years at Princeton, found him reacting with
high emotion:

> I burn, I hasten to engage
> To vent my poison with a serpent's rage.

Politically (then at least) Philip was a Whig or "liberal."
Among his special friends in this group was a thin, frail
Virginian, James Madison, whose brilliance of mind and

quickness of wit were a delight to his intimates and whose friendship with Thomas Jefferson in years to come proved invaluable to Philip. Another of Freneau's Princeton cronies was the exceptional Hugh Henry Brackenridge, a future distinguished jurist, who shared Philip's hunger for authorship. Together they labored over a novel, of which only fragments exist, and they could thank Witherspoon's Presbyterian Lord that this work escaped publication. But their joint authorship of the 1771 commencement poem does survive. It was entitled "The Rising Glory of America."

Those who believed that Witherspoon protected his "boys" from worldly upheavals simply did not know their man. Moreover, Witherspoon loathed William Franklin, the last of New Jersey's royal governors, who (as Witherspoon well knew) plotted to transform Princeton into an Anglican institution.

Why Freneau was listed on the 1771 commencement program as "necessarily absent" is confusing—in all likelihood, he ran out of cash—but Freneau's definitive biographer, Lewis Leary,* captures the impact upon the "vast concourse of the politest company" who gathered in Nassau Hall to hear the commencement poem Philip had written in collaboration with Hugh Brackenridge:

". . . A patriotic poem in the deepest sense, 'The Rising Glory of America' is a prophecy of the time when the standard of England shall wave from the Atlantic to the Pacific. It pictures a mighty nation of the future whose loyal subjects, 'warm in freedom's cause,' glory in their English heritage. Commerce, agriculture, and science were the pillars on which colonial prosperity was to be erected. The Indians were pictured as a savage race whose only salvation lay in peaceful submission to the wise and kindly rule of their Eng-

---

*Lewis Leary, *That Rascal Freneau* (New Brunswick, N.J., 1941), pp. 34–35.

lish conquerors. 'Britannia's warlike troops, choice spirits of her isle,' were celebrated with rapt sincerity. . . ."

No sentiments could have harmonized better with the thoughts of the audience in Nassau Hall. The prospect of a revolutionary war was furthest from their minds. They were Englishmen in America who expected to be treated with the same respect and freedom as Englishmen in the mother country (with the possible exception that they preferred Presbyterianism to Anglicanism in calming the savage breast).

Philip was at loose ends and as unhappy in farm life as ever his father had been. Then, as later, he may have been down to "not a brass farthing." By some stroke of luck he obtained a position as tutor among the wealthy Dutch on "Long Island"; the truth was that he endured just thirteen days in Flatbush before bidding adieu, as he wrote Madison, to "all its brutish brainless crew . . . void of reason and of grace"; but other troubles, doubtlessly involving salary, led Philip's employers to threaten "that if I was caught in New York they would either Trounce or maim me."

President Witherspoon good-humoredly allowed former students to lodge without charge in Nassau Hall as long as they continued their studies. Philip found the refuge attractive, whether eluding angry parents in Flatbush or the dullness of farm life at Mount Pleasant. Some say that in memory of his pledge to his father he turned to lessons in theology, but little evidence supports this theory. We do know that when this voluntary sojourn at Princeton ended he published under his own name in pamphlet form the verses of "The American Village," which, as he wrote Madison, was "damned by all good and judicious judges." His 450 lines, highly imitative of Pope, Goldsmith and others, deserved to be roundly criticized.

Hugh Brackenridge in the autumn of 1772 became a

licensed parson and master of Somerset Academy at Black Creek near Princess Anne, Maryland. He named Philip assistant master—with fatal results. "This is the last time I shall ever enter into such a business, it worries me to death and by no means suits my 'giddy wandering brain,' " Freneau wrote Madison. The Virginian would not recognize him in his reduced circumstances, Philip said—not with his hair "grown like a mop" and his "huge tuft of Beard." His noodle still meditated songs, more bitter than tuneful; and he did not win friends by proclaiming "May the Pope, or Roman Pontiff, be put into a pillory; and may the Devil pelt him with Priests."

But the time quickly approached when America could use a poet.

5

John Yankee vs.
John Bull

*Representing the years of the Revolution, William M.
Runyon stepped forward, resplendent in a sash of
thirteen stars. At two o'clock in the morning of April
24, 1775, express riders galloped into New Brunswick
with news of the fighting at Lexington and Concord.
"Trying times" followed "during those dark days of
1776–7" when the British occupied the surrounding
countryside. The last of these years brought fighting
to Piscataway and Bonhamtown [events that failed to
budge Washington's army from its refuge in the New
Jersey mountains and led to Brandywine, Germantown,
Valley Forge and Lord Howe's occupation of Philadelphia *]. Master Runyon described how the British
left New Brunswick and Amboy, burning houses as they
departed. In Piscataway alone 131 persons had been
plundered and thirteen buildings burned.*

Philip Freneau had fallen on golden times, for newspapers
everywhere sought patriotic poetry. Philip hedged, uncer-
tain that a war was necessary, and in *The American Whig*
lamented that

---

* The author described how the Revolution affected New Jersey in *Crossroads of Freedom* (New Brunswick, N.J., 1971) and does not intend to repeat
himself in these pages.

Englishmen, of all mankind,
Are the bravest and most blind.

Yet when New York City's liberty pole, a beautiful red
hickory of seventy-five feet, was destroyed, Philip's spleen
stirred:

Let them advance, by night and day,
Let them attempt a new affray,
And speedy vengeance will ensue,
  —*At least their hides beat black and blue.*

Philip's uneasiness lingered, however. He prayed for
some miracle by which George III could end the conflict so
that the country could grow harmoniously "from ocean's
edge to Mississippi's streams." But like so many who hesi-
tated Philip realized finally that George III *wanted* war.
Freneau responded angrily:

To arms, to arms, and let the trusty sword,
Decide who best deserves the hangman's cord.

But Philip at twenty-two had changed little from the sixteen-year-old boy who had entered Princeton. Farming, the
clergy, teaching, the Revolution—he did not seem to fit in
with any of them. Who was he to turn on George III if
Myles Cooper, the learned president of King's College
(Columbia), could remain loyal? He came at last to a
decision:

In distant isles some happier scene I'll choose,
And court in softer shades the unwilling Muse.

So Philip turned to the sea. "The Poet of the American
Revolution" was running out on his own war.

The decade that included the first years of the Revolution were boom times in Tuckerton. Often at nightfall as many as thirty ships could be counted at anchor in this port on Little Egg Harbor. Dutch vessels came seeking sassafras, a main ingredient in a popular Dutch drink called *sloop*. As a port of entry Tuckerton's customs-house employed a busy staff. Numerous industries clustered around the town—lumbering, shipbuilding, glassworks, charcoal manufactures, bog-iron furnaces, saltworks, castor oil production.

The Revolution simply made good times better in Tuckerton. In the spring of 1777 local privateersmen captured the British merchantmen, the *Venus* and the *Major Pearson*. These vessels, large and valuable, were captured off Sandy Hook and taken into the Mullica River through Old Inlet—a cheeky business, considering the number of Loyalist spies who roamed the Jersey seacoast. The cargoes were unloaded, the ships stripped clean, their equipment sold at public auction. The hulls were burned. In August, 1778, colonial newspapers, like the *New Jersey Gazette,* openly boasted: "Lately taken and brought into Little Egg Harbor (Tuckerton) by two New England privateers in company with Captain John Rice, a brig and a sloop loaded."

Such captures, the British well knew, helped to supply Washington at Valley Forge, and, anxious to find a scapegoat after their disastrous defeat at Saratoga, they replaced Lord Howe in command with Sir Henry Clinton. To end this hit-and-run warfare at sea Clinton organized a fleet of nine ships-of-war (about seven hundred men) under the flagship *Zebra.* Washington, warned of the move by his own spies, dispatched express riders to Tuckerton. Vessels disappeared from Little Egg Harbor like puppet ships suspended on strings. Meanwhile Count Casimir Pulaski, the Polish cavalryman who entertained guests by galloping full tilt, firing his pistol, then, twirling it in the air and catching the weapon before it touched the ground, was sent with his own special legion to re-enforce Tuckerton.

The entire region was in motion as local riders spread the alarm. Men hastily dug breastworks to protect Tuckerton. Women and children hid in the woods. Meanwhile the British armada anchored off the bar at Brigantine. Sailors searched the coast for someone who could pilot them in and captured Nathaniel Cowperthwaite. The deal probably was settled with a sword at Nathaniel's throat, for he was a stubborn patriot.

Still, Nathaniel held his tongue while he plotted revenge. He knew the tides and so piloted the enemy that as night fell two of the British vessels, the *Granby* and *Greenwich,* were hopelessly grounded. A chuckling Nathaniel dove overboard. Musket balls peppered the water around him, but Nathaniel, an excellent swimmer, soon reached safety.

British anger brought swift retaliation. Fire destroyed the village of Chestnut Neck on the Mullica River. Other houses were burned along the Bass River, a saltworks was wrecked, a mill razed, and about thirty prize boats were sunk. British forces landed on Osborn's Island, which was reckoned as four miles from Tuckerton. A sentinel (who could have been a Tory spy) led them to Pulaski's picket guard. The date was October 15, 1778, late at night.

A horrible scene followed. The British fell upon sleeping Americans. Cutlasses slashed throats and blood reddened the ground as thirty or more of the count's men died. The Redcoats tore up a bridge to ensure their escape. But Pulaski with his dark eyes flashing and his high brow turning pink became a fearful sight. With the main body of his legion he was hard on the heels of his attackers. Shots dotted the night's retreat. The British were close to the water and in a panicky mood. They ran for their flagship, the *Zebra,* which was now aground.

To save the flagship from capture torches were put to

her sails and timbers. Flames danced in the sky, and many
Britons died. Cheers within Tuckerton signaled the town's
salvation.

Ever since I was a child I have experienced a shivery feeling about that sparsely settled sandy region known as the
Jersey Pines. I saw it as a wasteland where witches lived in
gingerbread houses. The section's reputation certainly did
not improve during the Revolution with the depredations
of Tory Pine Robbers under desperadoes like Giberson and
his sister. This agile lady, we are told, could stand empty
barrels side by side and jump from one into the other without touching the rims. A trail of cold-blooded murders followed this pair.

John Bacon and his Tory thugs also were locally prominent, especially for their bloody misdeeds around Manahawkin. On October 25, 1782, a British cutter, bound for
the Dutch Indies from Ostend, grounded on Barnegat
Shoals, celebrated locally as the "Graveyard of the Atlantic." Patriotic Captain Andrew Steelman of Cape May discovered this derelict. In stripping the vessel of its cargo,
Steelman could imagine how delightful to colonial palates
the Hyson tea would taste. Steelman's crew had not finished
by nightfall and slumbered, exhausted, among the sand
dunes. Bacon and his Tory rascals could not resist an opportunity like this. In a sloop, ridiculously named the *Hero's
Revenge,* they sailed across the bay. "The Massacre of
Long Beach Island" was rightly titled. Knives stabbed the
hearts of Steelman's sleeping men. Others were shot, including the captain. Only five of twenty-five men escaped. Those
who cried for quarter were answered by malicious laughter.
Hatred for Bacon reached even to the governor, who offered £50 for his capture. A troop of Burlington County
militia marched off to bag the outlaw. Bacon waited in
ambush at the bridge across Cedar Creek and slaughtered

several militiamen. Stoically the local soldiers came on. They cornered Bacon in an inn between Weste Cunk and Clamtown (both in Tuckerton). With slashing sword, Bacon beat his way out of the place. On the porch stood Captain John Stewart, rifle to his shoulder. One shot felled Bacon.

Tory raiders operated along the length of the Jersey coast, although none outclassed "Bloody John" Bacon. William Dillon stalked men-of-war and merchantmen from Sandy Hook to Cranberry Inlet. Dillon's men left many a patriot dangling lifeless from a tree. Captain of the Associated Loyalists, which organized the labors of the raiders, was William Franklin, the last of the State's royal governors.

What a disappointment and trial William must have been to Benjamin Franklin! Reputedly the "natural son" of Benjamin and his common-law wife, Deborah Read,* he was carefully raised in his father's household. The boy fought the French on the New York frontier and rose to the rank of captain. A proud father boasted of Will at nineteen as "much of a Beau," but Benjamin could not ignore the youth's "Habit of Idleness" and hoped he would "apply himself to Business." Through Benjamin's obvious influence William became comptroller of the General Post Office and clerk of the Pennsylvania Provincial Assembly.

When in 1757 Benjamin Franklin went to England as agent for Pennsylvania and New Jersey, Will was his traveling companion. In London the youth attended Middle Temple and was admitted to the bar. In 1762 Oxford conferred the D.C.L. on the distinguished Benjamin and as a courtesy to his father made William a Master of Arts. William could be called handsome and was much courted by British society. This fact doubtless led to his undoing for,

---

* Another theory makes him the bastard of a maid.

as Benjamin told Thomas Jefferson, Will saw "too much
through the eyes of the [British] government."

There was not a wisp of Benjamin's democratic pragma-
tism in William. During the Revolution they split as neatly
as a log under an ax blow. William scored the Provincial
Congress of New Jersey as "an enemy to the liberties of
this country" and was exiled to Connecticut. There can be
no question that he was handled roughly and even denied
an opportunity to see his wife. In 1778 an exchange was
arranged, and William became president of the Board of
Associated Loyalists, in which he was assisted by Cortlandt
Skinner, the last royal treasurer, whose Tory raiders
burned and plundered many parts of Middlesex and Somerset counties. Within two years William was tired of the job
and returned to England, where he lived on an annual pension of £800.

Philip Freneau, probably to his own surprise, found the
West Indies as exotic as his father had said. Santa Cruz
was "inexpressibly beautiful." A mile from shore he believed that he was still sailing over the "blue, bottomless"
floor of the main ocean. Then, approaching land, the water
shallowed. Sponges and seaweed appeared. Philip looked
at the angelfish—"streaked over with circles near a half
an inch in breadth, which glow with all the lustre of the
most brilliant diamonds." He glanced upward at the cultivated fields of an island "cutting each other every way at
right angles." The sugar cane was "a most lively green."

Philip was "inexpressibly" enchanted. He looked down
at villages that captured his heart. Mango and orange
groves surrounded the homes of the planters. Philip found
his enthusiasm unshaken by a hurricane, for, he wrote, "a
continual solitude and silence reigns here." The tumult of
the world seemed far removed and Philip thought: "Happy

the Man who could pass his days in these extremities in peace and retirement."

But Philip recognized one flaw in his paradise—the slavery of the West Indian Negro. He became "melancholy and disconsolate." There was no pleasure in the world without its share of pain. He witnessed a Jamaica funeral and wrote:

> Like insects busy in a summer's day,
> We toil and squabble to increase our pain,
> Night comes at last, and, weary of the fray,
> To dust and darkness all return again.

Philip tried to complete his escape in the West Indies. He asked: "Absence and death . . . why should they cloud the sunshine of my mind?" But the truth struck him heavily: Washington driven across the Hudson, battle upon the fields of his own beloved Princeton, defeat at Brandywine and Germantown, the British occupying Philadelphia. On July 9, 1778, he reached Shrewsbury, ten miles from his native Mount Pleasant:

> Returned, a captive to my native shore,
> How changed I find the scenes that pleased before!

Six days later Philip became a private under Captain Barnes Smocks in the 1st Regiment of New Jersey militia. He was set to scouting and guarding a twenty-mile stretch of coast between South Amboy and Long Branch. His dog Sancho was his faithful attendant in these patrols that produced no enemy more malicious than mosquitoes until one night when Sancho suffered a saber-cut wound in the head during an assault and robbery near the Navesink Hills. Privateering—or piracy sanctified by war—was so popular that volunteers, Philip said, were "as plenty as grass-hoppers in the field." He filled the press of Philadelphia and

New York with poetic praise for these sea rovers and in late October became captain of the *Indian Delaware,* a schooner bound from the Shrewsbury River to Philadelphia and St. Eustacia in the West Indies. He collected two thousand dollars in merchandise in four months. He lost count after a time of the "several private sea fights" in which he participated but for the remainder of his life carried a bullet in his knee as a souvenir of these engagements.

December 30, 1779, was a memorable night. Gales uprooted trees along the Jersey coast. A rich British brig, the *Britannia,* was carried by the ice floes almost to Middletown Point. Philip was one of the militia under Captain Asher Holmes, who made the capture. Wind whipped along the road; the swirling snow stung like stone pellets. Eighty British crewmen were captured, and the ship's cargo—even to her sails, riggings and strips of copper bottom—was publicly auctioned by the Court of Admiralty. Irish beef, bread, coffee and sugar brought spirited bidding, perhaps more so than the *Britannia's* assortment of arms. Philip's share of the prize money came to $800 Continental money, the only official pay he received during the Revolution.

Philip's old college chum, Hugh Brackenridge, started publishing *The United States Magazine* in Philadelphia, and Freneau quit for a time his life as a sailor and soldier. His "The British Prison-Ship" scorned Tories who, like "blood hounds of some murderous line," preyed "like famished wolves upon their country." He delighted in picturing George III as a moral weakling. He paraphrased the speeches of England's Charles Fox, who believed his country ignored her closer and deadlier enemies:

> When France and Spain are thund'ring at your doors,
> Is this the time for kings to lodge with whores?
> In one short sentence take my whole advice,
> (It is no time to flatter or be nice)

> With all your soul for instant peace contend,
> Thus shall you be your country's truest friend.
> Peace, heavenly peace, may stay your tottering throne,
> But wars and death and blood can profit none.

Brackenridge's magazine foundered for need of money. Philip returned to privateering, preferring the groves of the West Indies to another blustery winter in New Jersey. The adventure all but cost Philip his life. His ship, the *Aurora,* was run down by the British man-of-war, *Iris,* bearing thirty-six guns and towing two American prize ships. The *Iris,* Philip said, "hulled us several times," and "one shot [that] went betwixt wind and water" caused the *Aurora* to leak "amazingly." Philip's claims that he was a mere passenger produced laughter. His name appeared on the *Aurora*'s gunners' list.

Philip was incarcerated in the British prison ship *Scorpion,* and, when he came down with fever, was transferred to the hospital ship, *Hunter,* which hardly proved to be any improvement:

> Such food they sent, to make complete our woes,
> It looked like carrion torn from hungry crows,
> Such vermin vile on every joint were seen,
> So black corrupted mortified, and lean.

Philip endured to "hang them up to infamy in song." He was released, intimately aware now that "war's clouded winter chills the charms of May"; and he mocked his enemy by having the royal governor of South Carolina declare:

> Though a brute and a dunce, like the rest of my clan,
> I can govern as well as most Englishmen can.

Cornwallis' surrender at Yorktown indicated that, no matter how much longer the war continued, George III

could not win. Freneau was asked to write a prologue to
the celebration honoring George Washington at Philadelphia's Southwark Theater. Philip revived his dream of a
future America:

> Even here where freedom lately sat distrest,
> See, a new Athens rising in the west;
> Fair science blooms where tyrants reign'd before,
> Red war reluctant leaves our ravag'd shore—
> Illustrious hero, may you live to see,
> These new republics powerful, great and free;
> Peace, heaven born peace, o'er spacious regions spread,
> While discord sinking veils her ghastly head.

6

Let My People Go

*Harold B. Van Horn wore a sash dated 1799, and
sixteen stars replaced the original thirteen. Citizens
went to New Brunswick for their mail since this "postoffis" received all the mail for Scotch Plains, Amboy,
Cranbury, Bonhamtown, Millstone, Basking Ridge,
"etc." A riding-chair, a chaise, or a gig "having two
wheels and wooden springs," was the conveyance
seen most often lined up before the post office. "If,"
Harold Van Horn said, "you had receivd a letter,
you would have had to pay the postage upon it, and
probably it would have been two shillings or more.
You would have red the letter many times, and past
it around for your friends and neighbors to read.
Then, with a quill pen made of a goose feather, you
would have written your reply to it; or else would have
askt the schoolmaster to write for you what you
wanted said, and you would, of course, have given
him a handsome present for doing so important a
piece of work for you." New Brunswick by now had
become a city with many stores and a newspaper. Its
markets sold almost everything, from a pair of knee
buckles to a Negro slave.*

The rebuffs of childhood are difficult to forget or forgive.
Between Asbury Park and Ocean Grove, that citadel of
Methodism where on Sunday no automobile could drive,

was a beach restricted to Negroes only. I could not understand the restriction, since during those earliest years of the twentieth century I had wet my toes in almost every inch of undulating waves from Long Branch to Asbury Park.

"Why can't I go on that beach?" I asked my mother furiously.

"Because you're white."

"What difference does that make?"

"Some day you'll understand," Mother said indulgently. "Now let's find the booth where you can have all the lemonade you can drink for ten cents."

"Or puke it up."

A person who stayed in a hotel in Asbury Park was a vacationer; if you stayed in a house in Ocean Grove you were a "cottager." The Methodists ran their resort as though it bordered on heaven. Even the milkmen appeared to walk on tiptoe. A resolute child (at least), I crept out of our lodging at dawn. At the beach reserved for Negroes I removed my shoes and stockings. Blissfully I walked through the sand to the ocean. Cold water curled around my toes, but I grinned despite chattering teeth. I dashed back to the boardwalk. A policeman awaited me.

"Boy, you've broken the law."

"What harm could I do putting my white feet in God's ocean?"

The policeman considered. "Damned if I know, son," he said, placing a gentle hand on my shoulder. "It beats me."

New Jersey's attitude toward its black citizens was haphazard. At the outbreak of the Revolution Shrewsbury required Negroes to turn in guns and other weapons "until the present troubles are settled" (in New Hampshire blacks were grouped with idiots and lunatics). In 1773 New Jersey's lower house imposed a duty of £20 on every imported slave, but the Council rescinded the tax. Negroes were restricted from the New Jersey militia in 1779, but slaves were allowed to serve as substitutes for their masters in the Continental forces, and their owners found the arrangement quite satisfactory in claiming land bounties. Slaves were freed whenever Loyalist land-holdings were seized.*

During the Civil War all eighteen slaves living in the Union resided in New Jersey, although in fairness to the State the fact should be mentioned that its freed slaves totaled 25,318. The unfortunate eighteen slaves were unaffected by the Emancipation Proclamation, since New Jersey was not at war with the Federal government, and their freedom was not won until the adoption of the Thirteenth Amendment.

Now in the age of the sons of the sons who were responsible for this achievement we retained ugly, unsuspected prejudices. We saw a segregated beach not as an insult to the Negro but as a personal annoyance. Ethnic humor toward all immigrants was commonplace and often extremely cruel. When Jess Willard dethroned Jack Johnson, Negro world heavyweight champion, my father hailed a new day when every "damned husky jigaboo" he met would not try to shove him into the gutter. Blacks lived in sections, usually the least desirable property in the community. Mother could not resist cuddling Negro babies, but she invariably called them "pickaninnies." Chapters of the Ku Klux Klan became popular in New Jersey during the 1920's.

We discovered that, if you did not think about a problem, it went away. When through exceptional ability a Negro excelled, we somehow took secret credit for that success. In high school we were proud of John Morrow, who became

* Benjamin Quarles, *The Negro in the American Revolution* (Chapel Hill, N.C., 1961), pp. 17, 41, 52*n*, 59, 70, 185.

ambassador to Guinea and the United Nations. His sister taught in the elementary school system, a tribute to our tolerance. And we adored Goven Mills, a Negro star on whom Hackensack depended to defeat its arch football rival, Englewood.

Surprisingly, in the early 1930's, New Jersey's principal idol was a Negro. The son of a Princeton minister, Paul Robeson had graduated from Rutgers University in 1919. Twice Walter Camp had named him All-American end. He was a member of Phi Beta Kappa and valedictorian of his class. Once each year he returned to the campus as a performer in the University Concert Series. His appearance was considered the event of the winter months. Sometimes students told their friends, more than half jokingly, "I go to Rutgers—you know, Paul Robeson's school."

Classmates who appeared to greet Robeson on concert day were outwardly jovial, but among themselves undertones of jealousy and perhaps of guilt tinged their conversation. It was not true, they said, that half the squad had threatened to resign if he were invited to the preseason football camp at Eatontown. Many muttered: "I never saw anyone deliberately step on his hands during scrimmage. I know I never did." If Robeson did not make the college glee club, it was because he did not try (which was true since he knew what a sore thumb he would seem at the dances that followed the concerts). Few would believe that the college president never said hello to Robeson when they met on a campus pathway.

Robeson was a magnificent figure standing six feet, three inches in height, or just one inch shorter than Abraham Lincoln. One of his ancestors, some said, had been king of an African tribe. A quick infectious smile was his mask against small, nagging adversities. After Rutgers he studied law at Columbia. His buoyancy of spirit, his extraordinary intellect, and his diversity of talents won many friends and brought him to the Provincetown Playhouse in Greenwich Village, where an old Princeton dropout, Eugene O'Neill, was writing the plays upon which his fame largely rested.

Unhappily, casting Robeson in the lead of *All God's Chillun Got Wings* was not a fortunate selection. In this drama O'Neill captured the tragedy of a black man who married a white woman and did so with such compelling insight that a good part of his audience was repelled. The recently revived chapters of the Ku Klux Klan in the metropolitan area threatened O'Neill and his family if the play were continued. The mayor's office decided that child actors could not perform in a play of such social controversy. Wherever Robeson turned, he was subjected to indignities.

O'Neill's Irish blood would not buckle under to the bigots. He wrote a new play for Robeson, *The Emperor Jones,* which Paul played in London. In England Robeson encountered none of the racial tension which had marred his acting career in Greenwich Village. He made a number of appearances on the concert stages of Europe before he returned to the United States and became the star of the musical comedy, *Show Boat.*

It was this Robeson, at the height of his fame, whom I knew at Rutgers. Annually his concerts filled the gymnasium. Season subscribers to the concert series occupied the main floor. "Robey's people" sat in the tiers in the balcony.

Slowly the lights dimmed until Robeson appeared, awesome and majestic, standing in the center of a single spotlight. He nodded to Lawrence Brown, his lifelong accompanist. When Robeson began to sing, his deep, enthralling baritone voice had a magical, uplifting quality. Throats choked and tears moistened many eyes. His rendition of

"Old Man River" brought the audience to its feet, cheering and applauding.

But that part of the program which Robeson devoted to his own people gave the auditorium almost the atmosphere of a cathedral. Robey's head was thrown back now, his voice reached out toward those in the upper balcony. The plaintive sweetness of "Li'l Gal" drew smiles and rumbling applause. His renditions of "Swing Low, Sweet Chariot," "Water Boy" and "Joshua Fit the Battle of Jericho" were the music of his people—music that he felt with all his being. Who could better understand the true meaning of "Sometimes I Feel Like a Motherless Child" or "Nobody Knows the Troubles I've Seen"? Unashamedly handkerchiefs wiped away tears. And heart continued to communicate with heart as he continued:

> . . . Go down, Moses,
> Way down in Egyp' Lan',
> Tell ol' Pharaoh
> To let my people go.

The social disruptions of the Great Depression, the factories that stood idle while their machinery rusted, the "sit-down" strikes and shop windows broken by bricks were among the many causes that led a growing majority of Americans to believe that an international conspiracy existed to destroy their way of life. Robeson was summoned before a Senate investigating committee and asked if he were a communist. In the sound belief that this query constituted an invasion of his privacy, Robeson refused to answer, and, although later he reputedly signed an affidavit that he was not a communist, very few believed him because, in their opinion, only a communist hid his true political identity behind "due process of law" or some trick phrase from the Bill of Rights.

Robeson's belief that a renaissance of Negro art and culture was desperately needed added to the feeling against him, for intellectuals, at the very least, were classified as "pinkos." Only intimate friends understood what Robeson suffered. When, giving a concert in an upstate New York University Club, the color of his skin forced him to ride in the freight elevator, he must have felt bitter at his exclusion from the freedoms provided by the Declaration of Independence. Certainly when he was made to choose carefully a restaurant where he might dine with his own son, he had cause to reflect bitterly upon the statement that "all men are created equal."

With the coming of the Second World War, Robeson's outspoken pro-Russian feelings were remembered. His classmates at Rutgers, freed of their jealousy and guilt, treated him as a Benedict Arnold. They suggested, none too subtly, that stories about the Negro's being roughed up during football practice were all lies. Letters from older alumni asked that Robeson's name be expunged from the University's rolls, but a committee of younger and sounder minds prevailed and he was not exposed to this insult. Beginning in 1950, Robeson became involved in an eight-year struggle to obtain a passport to leave the United States: the government believed him to be too dangerous a communist to turn loose on the remainder of the world. In June, 1958, he was granted travel privileges and left for a triumphant Soviet concert tour. Two years later he attempted a short tour of Australia and New Zealand, but his strength had played out and he returned to America to live his declining years in privacy.

During these closing years a Robeson revival has begun. At the Rutgers campus in Newark, Paul Robeson Plaza was dedicated in tribute to one of the University's most illustrious graduates. Recently a major recording company released an album of "Paul Robeson: Songs of My People," calling it "his legendary first Victor recordings."

Anyone whose intellect was honed to a point where he could feel compassion for a fellow-being grieved for Robeson when, at the zenith of his artistic achievement, he was driven to other shores. He stood alone, and his pain was invisible. Yet Robeson was equally the product of his environment, the classmates and friends, the professors and events that created his experiences. That so many of his colleagues were so deeply envious they could forsake him was shocking. His anger can only be imagined; his frustration must have been as bitter as gall.

Yet the aging man who came home, weary of the never-ending war for human justice, had won more than he suspected. Minds were opening, prejudices becoming recognized, the enormous dimensions of the problem understood. During the Centennial Celebration of the Civil War, a member of the New Jersey Commission, a Negro woman, was refused lodging in a southern hotel. The New Jersey Commission boycotted the meeting, supported by the unanimous resolutions of both houses of the New Jersey Legislature. President John F. Kennedy shifted the meeting to the Charleston Naval Base, where members of all races could attend.

7

Utopia in New Jersey

Miss Margaret A. Drake wore a sash of twenty-six stars. She could have recited her narration in one prolonged breath: "Seventy years ago [1839], wonderful things had happened. There was a daily steamboat line between New Brunswick and New York. A railroad had been built thru this place, and people could travel by train as fast as twenty miles an hour. A little light engin having only one driving wheel and burning, not coal, but wood, drew a train of queer little low cars over a single track. There was a station here [since demolished] cald Baptist Roads, and there was a new church, too, larger than the old one."

In the spirit of Miss Drake's narration, history had been moving with the speed of a flaming meteor after climactic factions began to develop among the members of President George Washington's official family. Thomas Jefferson believed that no man should owe constant obedience to an overlord any more than he should be bound by a perpetual constitution or a perpetual law. Since Jefferson declared that all wars were caused by men of commerce, his friction with Alexander Hamilton, the financier with the heart of a monarchist, became inevitable. John Adams, who never recovered from his excessive anti-Britishness, told his colleagues that, if they would behave like devout New Englanders, not much harm would ever overtake them. Washington based the wrangling within his cabinet largely upon one individual: "That rascal Freneau!"

The heart of James Madison must have twitched with guilt, for he had remembered his old Princeton classmate from Mount Pleasant, New Jersey, and had persuaded Jefferson to offer Freneau, a stanch republican, a position as translator in the Department of State. In the spring of the year Philip was extremely stand-offish about the matter, since Jefferson's post paid a miserly sum of $250 a year. Meanwhile, Madison induced another Virginian ex-Princetonian, "Light Horse Harry" Lee, to rally Freneau to the aid of the cause of republicanism. Philip considered starting a country newspaper, but his rural retreat in New Jersey hardly seemed a suitable place for publishing a weekly of national interest.

By fall, however, Philip placed hunger before his pride and accepted the position as translator in Jefferson's Department of State. Philip even enjoyed the jolly, clean bustle of Philadelphia, the new national capital. He began his days eagerly, striding the half-mile of High Street to where the State House fronted on Chestnut Street. The homes were well kept, the streets were arranged in neat rectangles, and willows, buttonwoods and poplars shaded the cobbled pavements.

Philip's labors in the State Department were quickly discharged each day, which was a lucky happenstance since Madison and Lee had found Freneau sound financial backing to edit a new weekly journal. Philip was like a man enraptured by a new mistress, and all of his passion was consumed in publishing the *National Gazette,* a paper that at all times was to be "truly republican in its principles and tendencies." His rivals were several. Philip proved agile in holding his ground in this battle of invective and abuse. His notes on Alexander Hamilton, whom Freneau considered a

would-be monarchist, were insultingly entitled "Court Para-
graphs." The Fourth of July was an occasion for Philip
to warn all citizens that they must jealously guard their
liberties:

>—watch each stretch of power,
>Nor sleep too soundly at the midnight hour,
>By flattery won, and lull'd by soothing strains.

Freneau supported the French Revolutionists, which
made Adams copper-red with indignation while pleasing
Jefferson. Under the pseudonym of Pomposo, Hamilton
wrote malicious attacks upon Freneau, who replied gaily:

>Pomposo's dull printer does nothing but fret;
>Now preaching
>And screeching.
>Then nibbling
>And scribbling,
>Remarking
>And barking,
>Repining
>And whining
>And still in a pet
>From morning till night with the Nation's Gazette.

Late eighteenth-century journalism was not noted for
its generosity, honesty, or fear of pistol duels at dawn. A
fictitious advertisement pictured Philip virtually on bended
knee as he implored the State Department for a position as
French translator "at extraordinary low wages, besides soul,
body and conscience surrendered to the absolute disposal of
government." The obvious opposition of Jefferson to Washington's policies scandalized conservatives. When Jefferson
appeared to be losing his grip as Secretary of State, he dis-
tracted attention from this plight by assaulting Hamilton's

fiscal policies. Remembering that Freneau once had used the nautical pen name of Captain Sinbat, his critics were merciless in flailing his association with Jefferson:

> Sinbat, the smutty link-boy of the muse,
> Who blacks himself to clean his master's shoes— . . .

Freneau categorized the anti-Federalists as toads that "sucked poison from the earth." Washington's re-election drew from Philip the judgment that not "even Cincinnatus" had "received adulation of this kind." War between England and France brought the American reaction that should have been expected—once more George III endangered human freedom. Washington well might wish that governmental quarrels could be kept within his official family, but Freneau had out-guessed him—freedom of man was nourished on public policy or democracy otherwise ceased to endure. When the first French frigate sailed up the Delaware, a banner attached to its rigging read:

> "Freemen Behold, We Are Your Friends and Brothers."

If under the circumstances Philip Freneau's coat puffed with pride until a button popped, that result should not have surprised anyone.

As a partner in a new nation New Jersey could not avoid the tussle of a dog-eat-dog world composed of many nations. Some dangers could be anticipated, even in a country not yet a century old, but others (usually those closest to home) could not. In 1837 the first of the inevitable depressions which accompany industrial revolution and capitalistic enterprises paralyzed the young nation. True, there had been forewarnings—banks closing in New York and Philadelphia—but the nation was still without skill in recognizing such portents of disaster. Soon no bank could meet a demand for payment in gold and silver. Stores, offices, factories hung "closed" signs on their doors; the wheat crop failed and the cost of flour sky-rocketed; boats with empty holds groaned against hawsers on . forsaken docks. Men with grim, lean faces roamed the streets of cities, towns and hamlets seeking employment.

Only twenty-four years after the voyage of Columbus, Sir Thomas More published *Utopia* (a name invented by combining two Greek words that meant "not a place").* Although More made no reference to Columbus, the utopia that he planned was apparently intended to be established somewhere in the West Indies. In the society of More's *Utopia* no one was either immensely rich or immensely poor. Everyone worked with his hands, but no one was permitted to labor more than six hours a day. At the same time marriage was not recognized as a suitable human institution. Actually More feared, if he did not really distrust, individuals, and under no circumstances would he grant freedom to such dangerous creatures. His utopia was a Roman Catholic monastery, where all individuality was hidden behind uniforms.

Still staggering under the blows of its first depression, Protestant America, though attracted to some degree of socialism, had to look elsewhere for a guide, and discovered him in the French social reformer, Charles Fourier.† Broken in health by various commercial enterprises, Fourier conceived of a new world which would be comprised of small co-operative groups—the phalanxes—consisting of about sixteen hundred people. Each phalanx would be au-

---

* Odell Shepard, "Utopia in America," *The American Story,* ed. by Earl Schenck Miers (New York, 1956), pp. 154–58.

† Jean Boorsch, "Fourier," *The Encyclopaedia Americana* (1963), XI, 550B. At its height, it is doubtful if Fourierism attracted more than 3,800 adherents. Its most notable convert was Napoleon III.

tonomous, self-sufficient, devoted to work and love "in an atmosphere of freedom, enthusiasm and harmony." Among those who espoused the ideas of Fourier, seeing great promise once they had been properly Americanized, was Horace Greeley, editor and publisher of the *New York Tribune,* who embraced such fads as phrenology and vegetarianism.

Perhaps the most ambitious of these organizations was the North American Phalanx, which stood on the road from Colt's Neck to Lincroft (then called Leedsville for the family who owned the property at the crossroads where the village ultimately developed). What remained of the once famous North American Phalanx, which my wife and I visited in 1969, was a row of five or six connected houses. An angry woman came down the drive, screaming: "Git out—git out!" Behind her stood a man with a double-barreled shotgun. We took flight, feeling like two innocents who had stumbled upon an illegal still.

We returned a few years later. Either fierce storms or lightning and fire had destroyed the remaining dwellings. Vines crawled up a single crumbling abutment. Atop sat a crow, looking lonely and forsaken. A yellow dog bared its teeth. We felt sad and hoped that someday the New Jersey Historical Commission would place a sign along the road:

In the Fields Beyond
Once Stood
Utopia
In New Jersey
1843–1855

To settlers in a region still being hacked from the forest primeval, the Phalanx must have been an awesome spectacle, spreading over an area of 673 acres, which cost the proprietors $14,000. The central building, occupied by the officers and directors, rose in one section to three stories. Columns supported a roof at ground level and offered protection in times of rain and snow. Connected wings were used as the dwellings and workshops of the communal members, and thus gave the impression of a phalanx, an ancient Greek military formation. Other structures included a granary, an ice house, a renovated chicken house, a carpenter's shop and buildings for various mechanical crafts. There was also a sawmill.

The appeal of the Phalanx was largely to members of the middle class. Among early investors in the community were a morocco manufacturer, a grocer, a shoestore proprietor, a coach-maker, a druggist, an agent for a transportation company, a dry-goods merchant, a painter, a secretary of an insurance company, a dealer in anthracite coal, a partner in a tobacco company, the owner of a steamship line, a physician, a stove dealer, and a lawyer.* Generally the Phalanx was composed of persons who had been private entrepreneurs victimized by the Depression of 1837 and were joined in the belief that since nature was "wild and untempered," and the individual unstable in his impulses, a proper balance between nature and civilization existed only in the concept of the supervised small village.

The Phalanx was not a welfare state, but rather a "hard money" organization. Members were expected to invest in the buildings they occupied; they received a monthly allowance for personal expenses, including clothing, "at as near net cost as convenient," and, if at the year's end a profit existed, they shared in the payment of bonuses. The amount of the original investment and the quantity of work produced in a year determined the size of the dividend, and many individuals prospered far more than their companions.

* For much of the information used in this section the author is indebted to Herman J. Belz whose senior thesis on the North American Phalanx is in the Princeton University Library.

Whereas the capitalistic axiom that the Lord helps those who help themselves became one of the factors in the ultimate demise of the Phalanx, there were other influences with greater effect on its unhappy future. The age was one when the majority of people were the sons or grandsons of the men who had fought the battles of the Revolution, and human freedom and dignity were principles close to their hearts. The paternalistic proprietors of the Phalanx took quite another view, denying the "radical" doctrine that all men were created equal. The Phalanx acknowledged only one obligation—to provide its members with "an adequate maintenance together with the best educational facility within its power." After all, the business of the Phalanx was not to produce philosophers or "people of literary taste," but to train individuals who could earn their livelihoods as brickmakers, ironworkers, tinworkers, blacksmiths, canners of fruits and vegetables, or from other crafts.

From the outset children had been a source of vexation to the Phalanx. A form of health insurance to protect the young in times of illness was voted down because, one of its founders said, such insurance would be like "forming a guarantee society within a guarantee society," yet acknowledging responsibility for orphan children "if they had not the means to care for themselves." The conflict between the social paternalism of the Phalanx and the sentiments of the individual toward his progeny culminated in a quarrel over whether a child's primary responsibility was with the family or society. There were those who confused the issue by arguing that society could not produce a child. But by 1854 the *Proceedings* of the Phalanx acknowledged as "a grave mistake" any concession to the proposition that society and not the parent should determine a child's development. To those who believed that the parent was

better suited to direct the child's education, the manage-
ment answered coldly that the very nature of its industrial
organization would quicken a child's progress in acquiring
crafts necessary for self-sufficiency.

There were disputes over religion. The attitude of the
Phalanx was that a person could take or leave religion,
according to his taste, but this agnosticism grated upon
people whose backgrounds were basically Christian. One
Eleazer Parmly, short-tempered and not afraid to show it,
turned his wrath upon the proprietors. All persons, he said,
who have any regard for the religion of the Bible should
reveal their outraged feelings by severing their connections
with the North American Phalanx. Parmly's indignation
resulted in the formation of a splinter group called "The
Raritan Bay Union," led by George Arnold and Marcus
Spring, which endorsed in every way the traditional tenets
of Christian belief and conduct.

To internal dissensions over children and religion was
added a fatal blow in the form of a fire that destroyed the
mill. The directors of the Phalanx recognized their complete defeat. Early in 1855 the doors of the Phalanx were
locked for the last time.

A half century later my uncle John McQueen, who ran
the family farm in Colt's Neck, could not mention the
Phalanx without an undertone of anger, as though somewhere down the Lincroft road lurked hidden enemies who
remained determined to destroy him. His mouth would
tighten in a straight line, and all at once I would notice the
tobacco juice stains on the edges of his moustache. Usually
they were not noticeable for my uncle possessed a peculiar
mouth and cheeks which seemed to puff out as though small
clouds of good cheer floated within. In contrast to his dis-
dain for the Phalanx, his head lifted proudly and he

whistled *Yankee Doodle* whenever we passed the battle-
fields of Monmouth on the road to Englishtown.

During World War I we lived in Brooklyn, New York,
and the golden seasons of these years were the summers,
when we migrated to the old family farm in Colt's Neck.
Even the prospect of a wearying, all-day journey did not
dull our enthusiasm. We traveled by steamboat from the
Battery at the tip of Manhattan Island to Red Bank, where
Uncle McQueen met us with the farm wagon for the
seemingly endless haul to the farm.

What a pity it is that the leisurely delight of traveling
by steamboat has largely disappeared. The boat on which
we embarked, the *Albertina,* was making an "empty run"
—that is, it was bringing back the baskets and crates in
which farm produce had been shipped to market the previous afternoon. As a result, the children had almost complete freedom of the boat. The crates, up-ended, provided
a fine course for leapfrog. There were nooks everywhere to
add excitement to games of hide-and-seek. We munched on
the sandwiches Mother had packed for lunch and washed
them down with the then popular soft drink, Moxie, which
always left me feeling nauseated. The wonders of the
Albertina to me were the brass rods that turned its paddle-
wheels. They were shined to a point where you could see the
reflection of your face, and as the rods moved your image
changed so that your nose became long and then short, your
chin disappeared and your mouth spread over it. It was like
being surrounded by the mirrors in some amusement-park
fun house.

The boat's whistle screamed as we turned for the landing
at Red Bank. Mother strained her neck and cried joyously:
"He's here, he's here!" Uncle McQueen waited patiently
in the farm wagon. He chewed a monstrous plug of tobacco
and squirted a stream out the side of his jaw as though

returning the welcome of the boat whistle. The two horses with their ears protruding through straw hats shied backwards. Every timber of the vessel seemed to tremble as the side-wheeler came around and the paddles churned forward and back. There were weird hissing sounds; and a deckhand shouted at the passengers, "Get the hell back of that line like it says you ought!" An angry old man in a white Panama hat waved his cane and threatened to thrash the deckhand within an inch of his life if he again used offensive language before the ladies present. Chivalry still survived in the early twentieth century.

Slowly, almost miraculously, the boat lined up before the dock pilings. The pilot pulled the cord for three toots. Gradually he slipped the steamer between the pilings without a bump. Chains were hooked in place on the dock. Winches whirred. The deckhand raised the barrier crying: "Youse can go now." With glittering eyes the old gentleman in the Panama hat led the group forward. He brandished his cane like a sword.

In the wagon Mother and Father shared the seat with Uncle McQueen. I could not see how Mother could endure kissing my uncle's tobacco-stained, moustachioed mouth, but then she held an affectionate attachment toward my uncle and Aunt Laura, who had cared for Mother after her widowed mother had died.

"Good day?" Father asked pleasantly.

Uncle McQueen slapped his pocket. "About three hundred dollars."

"Since you never reach home until after dark, aren't you afraid of being robbed?"

"Haven't been yet. But I've a loaded double-barreled shotgun hidden under the seat and I sure can surprise anyone who wants to try it."

Even then Uncle McQueen belonged to a world that was

vanishing, not only in Monmouth County but also in other rural areas of the State. He was one of that old and noble tribe of family farmers who huckstered from town to town the produce of their own labors. Once they had been the State's tower of strength; now, though they ignored the indications, they were being squeezed out. Potato farmers combined to hire roving bands of Jamaica blacks during the picking season. Other farms converted to dairying or poultry raising. Freehold, Monmouth's county seat, already had a canning factory. But there was too much of the Ulster Irish and Presbyterian tenacity in Uncle McQueen for him to change. He needed no Phalanx to run his life. He would live and die a small but independent entrepreneur.

My sister Didi (Edith) and I were stored in the back of the wagon with the half-baskets and crates of produce that had not sold that day. Didi complained of the straw that crept up her legs.

"You turn your head and look the other way while I brush it out," she said severely. Didi had invented modesty.

What a wonderful combination of odors surrounded us! I rested my head on a sack half-filled with onions. Like famished wolves we attacked the remains of a basket of peaches, then turned on the apples.

"Didi, did you ever suck a raw egg?"

"Ugh!"

"I don't think I'll try it either."

Along one side of the wagon was the shelf of condiments which Aunt Laura had canned and sold for her "pin money." Didi found the small jar of honey. "We could scoop it out with our fingers." Nodding, I almost broke my teeth loosening the top. Underneath was a layer of paraffin wax.

"Now what?" Didi asked.

"Break it," I said. "You can chew that wax like gum."

We were half sick when, fortunately, we fell asleep. We

awoke with a start. It was night and the wagon had turned into the lane to the farm. The moon was in its last quarter and the sky glittered with stars.

Aunt Laura, a small woman with a birdlike pertness and an alertness that could be mistaken for flightiness, began placing supper on the table. The room reverberated with shouted greetings. Adam, my uncle's one farmhand—a runaway German orphan who bore the scar on his cheek where an angry father had struck him with a heated poker —called my mother "Em" and my father "Bill." Aunt Laura's ancient, crippled father, Mr. Cromwell, jerked himself awake and muttered, "I must have been napping."

"For the fiftieth time today," Adam said unnecessarily.

Mr. Cromwell rested his chin on his cane and glowered at Adam. Something about the old man unnerved me. He liked to hook the handle of his cane under the belly of the cat and hoist the animal aloft, wriggling and howling. If Aunt Laura caught him, he was denied his glass of sherry at supper. Uncle McQueen returned from locking his money in the safe.

What a meal Aunt Laura served us. We had bean soup, chicken and dumplings, corn freshly pulled that afternoon, pickled beets and cucumbers, boiled white onions, milk and coffee with fresh cream, homemade butter and bread, and two kinds of pie. Mr. Cromwell apparently had behaved himself that day for he received his sherry.

A family farm in those days was a self-sufficient community, as elaborately organized and efficiently run as any phalanx. A rooster crowing at dawn sent Uncle McQueen and Adam off to their prebreakfast chores. There were cows to milk and eggs to collect and last night's swill to be carried to the pigsty. My uncle left one of the large milk cans beside Aunt Laura's butter churn on the back porch. The remainder went to the ice house, a dark and mysterious structure where the pond ice, cut in winter and stored under straw, supplied the summer's refrigeration. There was a separate tool house, an emery wheel with saddle and pedals for sharpening axes and scythes, a corncrib, and a long shelter for the wagons and farm equipment. The barn was bigger than the house and a door opened from the loft with a wheel and rope overhead that was used for hauling up hay in the appropriate seasons. Behind a white picket fence in the front yard paced a collie, awaiting the proper moment to bark at the man who delivered the rural mail. A pair of sheep kept the grass "clipped." A mile away stood the "new field" where Uncle McQueen raised his corn. Along the road to the cornfield tall chestnut trees cooled the sand under our bare feet. There was a brook here with overhanging sassafras trees. Didi chewed the bark almost incessantly and Mother worried.

But Father laughed. "It can't be too harmful, for somewhere I read that George Washington used a sassafras twig for a toothbrush."

"Most of his teeth fell out," Mother answered sharply.

There was as much gaiety as drudgery in farm life. The telephones then, large wooden boxes screwed to the wall, rang a number of times (up to six, as I remember) to indicate who was being called. But at the first ring everyone rushed to listen in. No child was born, no adult died, no marriage was arranged, no new recipe for pickles was discovered without the entire neighborhood's becoming immediately informed. On Wednesdays the butcher's wagon from Freehold arrived and Aunt Laura bought a leg of lamb or a roast of beef (usually she had "just" plucked two chickens for barter, which brought down the cost of meat considerably). Once a month the "notion man" drove down the road. Tin pots, pans and kettles clattered against the sides of his wagon. He also had strings of cowbells hung along each side.

"Fittin' to wake the dead," Mr. Cromwell grumbled. His wild-eyed gaze searched for the cat, which, luckily, was sunning in the backyard and swatting at chickens that came too near.

Anyone who was able-bodied worked on a farm. Even kids like Didi and me raked or hoed or picked beans or dug potatoes or kept the wood-box filled beside the mammoth iron kitchen stove or wavered on tremulous tiptoe while a garter snake slithered by, for Uncle McQueen had warned us never to harm "this friend of a farmer." There was fun, too. The favorite farmyard game was pitching horseshoes, at which Father was an expert. One day Adam pitched a ringer, which Father topped with another ringer, which Adam topped with a third ringer, which Father topped with a final ringer, giving him an exceptional victory. Adam was so enraged, he heaved the horseshoes over the roof of the barn.

"Now, you damn fool," my uncle said, "you can wade through the manure until you find 'em."

Father was an extremely strong man but doubted if he could throw those horseshoes over the barn roof, a confession which, for some reason, mollified Adam. Father talked of the cycling races of his youth—of which the century, or hundred-mile race, was the classic. Father competed in the shorter races of twenty-five miles and usually won. A powerful swimmer, he was the only one for miles around who had swum both directions of tidal Raritan Bay from its wide point at Keyport to Staten Island. And Mother would not allow Father to forget the time when he was driving a group of girls in a one-horse sleigh, cut one curve too sharply, and dumped his party in a snow-bank.

Saturday brought the greatest fun in the week, for then the farmers "went to market" in Freehold. The lane that led from Main Street to the selling lot was called Market

Alley and there for a nickel one could buy the biggest frank-
furter with sauerkraut in the world. Aunt Laura took her
"pin money" from the teapot on the top shelf of the breakfront in the dining room, cautioned Mr. Cromwell not to
tease the cat and fastened on a hat at least twenty years out
of style.

"Haven't you something newer than that?" Mother
asked.

"You don't throw away usable clothing on a farm," Aunt
Laura replied.

Father laughed. "The most astounding freak show on
earth," he said, "is Freehold on Saturday night."

I rode on the farm wagon that had taken my uncle and
Adam half a day to pack. We left toward nightfall. Father
drove the women in a surrey. Uncle McQueen devoted his
time to selling and swapping. Thus he gained a bunch of
bananas for two baskets of ripe tomatoes and a sack of
steamer clams for some lima beans and carrots. He was a
sharp bargainer, haggling over each exchange, and no deal
was settled until he dignified it with a stream of chewing
tobacco.

I went to join the others, knowing where to find them. For
Aunt Laura no trip to Freehold was complete without stopping at the confectionery store for a lemon phosphate. I
found my aunt, Mother and Didi sitting at a marble-topped
table on seats with intertwining curved wire backs. Overhead four fans spun so slowly that flies lit on the brownish
blades, and Didi insisted they mistook the fans for merry-
go-rounds.

The smells, sounds and sights of the stores of Freehold
on a Saturday night were unforgettable. What odor ever
surpassed that of a freshly opened barrel of gingersnaps or
the fragrance of roasted peanuts? What glass-front cases
were more entrancing than those filled with jars of pepper-
mint sticks, horehound drops, pinkish and crystal-clear rock

candy, Yucatan chewing gum, cinnamon "red hots," squares of maple sugar, and chocolates shaped like cigars? While the adults fingered bolts of dress goods and examined traps and rifles, my eyes feasted on toys, wooden soldiers, rag dogs and cats, and such store-bought games as lotto and tiddlywinks. A bone-handled Barlow knife with two blades was perfect for mumblety-peg.

We were late returning home, but next morning Adam and my uncle arose with the crow of the rooster. Sunday, of course, was special for its ice cream. Aunt Laura saved all the dead-ripe peaches, cutting out the brown spots; a gallon can with a paddle held a mixture of cream and peaches, which was placed in a tub packed with ice and rock salt; a big handle cranked the can until the cream had thickened. Sisters and brothers have become virtual enemies for life, fighting over who should have the first lick of the paddle. Mr. Cromwell pounded his cane, wanting his turn at the paddle. The finest invitation a neighbor could give was, "Come Sunday for dinner and we'll turn the crank."

The farm family enjoyed four special events. The Strawberry Festival in spring raised money for the church. A row of colored ribbons in the dining-room breakfront denoted the prizes Aunt Laura had won for her baked goods and canned relishes and my uncle had won for his vegetables, fruits and livestock at the County and State Fairs. But the spectacular days (adults, fifty cents; children over ten, twenty-five cents; all others, free) were those of the annual Harvest Home, another means of raising money for the church.

Aunt Laura baked pies for a week. Uncle McQueen "turned the crank." Adam picked the finest peaches, apples and grapes. Mother and Didi shelled lima beans and plucked chickens until their fingers ached. Father and I picked two crates of tomatoes—the red to slice, the green to fry. Mr.

Cromwell dozed, a smile on his face, likely dreaming of his youth.

Tables and benches filled the sloping front lawn of the Dutch Reformed Church. First came the near-endless blessing, thanking God for His bounteous harvests. The challenge at this point was to eat everything in sight. How gamely they stuffed, those farm people.

The noise grew incredible. Babies yelled, and women, accustomed to this cacophony, easily out-shouted them while exchanging local gossip. Men blustered over crops and the weather, prices and dwindling profits and how the world was spinning straight toward hell. Boys and girls raced between the benches, screamingly endeavoring to organize a game of hide-and-seek or a sack race. Adolescents sneaked off, looking for sequestered places where they could smooch without being observed by younger brothers and sisters.

Because of the reddish dust we kicked up, we were made to play behind the church. It was spooky, in a way, for a fence did not then divide the yard from the burial ground. A dirt lane led down to a circle and returned. A few faded flags still hung limply on the graves of veterans of the Civil War. When we played hide-and-seek the blasphemers who crouched behind the tombstones could stay there till they rotted, for all I cared.

With nightfall we drifted back to our families. A rope between two trees held a row of Japanese lanterns. Candles flickered within their multicolored sides; they were pretty. We sang favorite old hymns like "Rock of Ages" and "Nearer My God to Thee." The songsters were no more melodious than at any church service, yet ever since the first time we sang the impression has lingered that the farmer who works with his fingers in the earth touches hands with the Almighty.

8

Something More than Common

The graduates of the Class of 1909, Stelton Grammar School, had reached 1869, or forty years from the end of the three centuries of New Jersey history they were recalling, when William G. Dorward, wearing a sash with thirty-seven stars, stepped to the front of the platform. The time was one, he said, when the "telegraf" had come into use and people had begun to own sewing machines, mowers, reapers and horse-rakes. Master Dorward continued: "The Civil War was ended, and the monument in our churchyard testifies that Piscataway Township and this church were mourning for those of their sons who in that struggle had given their lives for their country. The company of soldiers who went out from Piscataway Township started with Rev. Christian J. Page, pastor of this church, as their captain, but when they took their place in the 28th Regiment of the New Jersey Volunteers, he became chaplain of the regiment, and Joseph Letson became captain of Company C."

The New Jersey Brigade, four regiments strong, was the first to reach Washington. The correspondent for the *New Jersey Mirror and Burlington County Advertiser* of Mount

Holly recalled with pride how in early May, 1861, the New
Jersey troops marched in full parade along Pennsylvania
Avenue. Thousands of spectators cheered the men as they
passed by in good step with rifles over their shoulders. The
correspondent reported: "They marched through the
grounds at the White House, where the President stood,
with hat in hand to receive them. He remarked that New
Jersey, according to her population, had presented a fuller
and more completely equipped body of men, than any other
State. Every man felt proud that he was a Jerseyan, and
especially a Jersey volunteer."

Next morning a band gathered at Willard's Hotel to sere-
nade Major Robert Anderson, defender of Fort Sumter, and
General Theodore Runyon, commander of the New Jersey
Brigade. Meanwhile the Commissary Department was busy
supplying the Jersey regiments "with cooking stoves, kettles,
wood, &c., &c." The meal that night consisted of a piece of
pork, four biscuits and a tin cup of coffee, a repast that the
reporter "relished." The troops camped in a field in Virginia and President Lincoln and Secretary of State William
Seward received "wild cheers" when they visited the bivouac. Some eight hundred men working in companies of fifty
cut down the pine trees "which obstructed the view in the
direction of the enemy."

In a letter to the *Trenton True American,* Lieutenant
F. S. Mills found the country "wretchedly poor" despite the
fact that the men were within sight of the Lee Mansion on
Arlington Heights. Officers who sought to have their clothes
washed were turned down by the poor whites who, apparently, had no knowledge of how to use soap, a scrubboard
and a bucket of water. Lieutenant Mills remembered: "We
found an old widow occupying a small house, opposite our
camp. To our surprise, we found her in possession of several barrels of whiskey; and very little else. She had some
tea and a few eggs. I paid a shilling for a cup of tea. As soon

as the whiskey was discovered, the old lady had a grand rush, so great that a guard of men had to be placed at the door. When the officers saw that the whole camp was about to get drunk, Gen. Runyon dispatched a soldier to tell her to sell no more; she continued to do so nevertheless, when the General sent some men to knock in the heads of the barrels. The old lady declared she was ruined." But the poor woman was quickly forgotten when within less than a month the New Jersey men moved to Roach's Springs, where they established Camp Princeton.

New Jersey's troops fought hard and well in every major battle of the next four tragic years. In books, unpublished diaries, and to a surprising extent in letters to their home-town newspapers they told a story of valor, sacrifice, and grim death. Great generals arose among their ranks—Philip Kearny, Judson Kilpatrick, Joseph Kargé, Gershom Mott and Robert McAllister.

Hinton Rowan Helper, a German-born author in North Carolina, who had made few friends when he had accused the South of selling its soul to the Devil for a bale of cotton, with equal candor called New Jersey "a second-rate free state." * Lincoln could not cope with the "Peace" Democrats and Copperheads who dominated New Jersey politics and lost the 1860 election by a plurality of more than six thousand. It was because Lincoln believed that somewhere en route to his Inaugural in Washington he must test the loyalty of "hostile country" that he decided to journey through New Jersey. That stout-hearted Quaker, Governor Charles S. Olden, had invited the President-Elect to include the State in his itinerary, thus "affording the citizens of New Jersey an opportunity to express the respect they feel for your character and position," and Lincoln had accepted,

---

* In 1861 Lincoln appointed Helper consul at Buenos Aires.

stipulating: "Please arrange no ceremony that will waste time." *

Naturally there were complications caused in no small part by the tremendous ovations Lincoln received in New York, and he was forced to decline the opportunity of resting at the home of John J. Chetwood of Elizabeth, even though Mr. Chetwood assured the President-Elect: "My house is large enough for you all, and you can be as retired as you wish. New Jersey, you know, is safe conservative ground." Lincoln, however, stuck to his schedule of journeying through New Jersey on Thursday, February 21, 1861, and reached the ferry depot at the foot of Courtlandt Street on what one poet described as the "perfect day" that had followed "in the pursuing brightness of ten thousand eyes" shining as the sun touched the surface of the Hudson River. An elegant new ferryboat, the *John P. Jackson,* gaily decorated with streamers, awaited Mr. Lincoln. There remained some confusion over whether the band was instructed to play "Hail to the Chief" or "Hail Columbia," and possibly it combined the two, for the crash of the music satisfied everyone. Governor Olden, who was in Washington representing the State at a "peace conference," was unable to greet the President-Elect and sent in his place Attorney General William L. Dayton, a man who so impressed Lincoln that he later appointed Dayton Minister to France. The pilot of the *John P. Jackson* could not resist changing his course so that his famous passenger could see Bedloe's Island. Two ships, the *Africa* and the *Jura,* belonging to the Cunard Line, fired a twenty-four-gun salute.

---

* David C. Mearns, Historian Emeritus of the Library of Congress, has written the best single account of Lincoln's journey through New Jersey in *Largely Lincoln* (New York, 1961), pp. 61–84. See also Earl Schenck Miers and C. Percy Powell, *Lincoln Day-by-Day* (Washington, D.C., 1960), III, pp. 19–20, and Roy P. Basler, ed., *The Collected Works of Abraham Lincoln* (New Brunswick, N.J., 1953), IV, 234–38.

Eventually the President-Elect reached Jersey City—or what Mayor Van Vorst called "Old Jersey"—and was greeted by A. A. Hardenbergh, president of the Board of Aldermen. The politician in Mr. Hardenbergh could not overlook an auspicious occasion for making a speech, but he finally ended, breathlessly, "Welcome, thrice welcome to the soil of New Jersey." The reporter from the *Philadelphia Inquirer* disclosed the somewhat startling information that Lincoln kissed a Miss Annie Smith, without mentioning that this irresistible lass was a babe in arms. Attorney General Dayton delivered an appropriate greeting on behalf of the governor, and in replying Lincoln revealed his admiration for the attorney general by declaring that "No state which possesses such a man can ever be poor."

A crowd of about twenty thousand, which cheered constantly and raucously, made it difficult to understand what anyone said. One broad-shouldered "son of Hibernia" succeeded in climbing aboard the platform to shake hands with Mr. Lincoln. His name was Mickey Free, and a policeman punched him in the nose. The crowd pushed and shoved, reluctant to let the President-Elect depart, and with good humor, bowing to the ladies in the gallery, Mr. Lincoln remarked that he was getting the better of this bargain.

The engineer tooted the train whistle as a signal that the time schedule was becoming tight. The band struck up another tune while Lincoln and his party slipped onto the special car reserved for them. The engine, the "Speaker Pennington," was decorated with a silken star on the front of its boiler, while its sides were trimmed with flags and flowers. One of the cars had been used to transport the Prince of Wales during a recent visit to New Jersey, but Mr. Lincoln was given a car that quite out-classed it. Small flags decorated the front and rear windows together with festoons and rosettes of the national colors. There were four lounges, two marble-topped tables and perhaps half a dozen ordinary chairs. A beautiful bouquet covered one table and, we are told, "shed fragrance on the air." The car was richly carpeted, and hot-air furnaces could be adjusted for even heat. The engineer sounded several shrill shrieks of the whistle, the locomotive began to puff and Mr. Lincoln at last was on his way to Newark.

Here new difficulties arose. In order to change from the "lower depot" of the Morris and Essex Railroad to an "upper station" on Chestnut Street, a ride by carriage of about a mile and a half along Newark's main thoroughfare was required. Since dawn people had been traveling from surrounding communities so that they might catch a glimpse of the "Illinois Ape" who had captured the White House. Some estimated the crowd lining Broad Street as large as seventy-five thousand, although reporters for sternly anti-Lincoln newspapers cut this figure to twenty-five thousand or less.

Lincoln rode in a barouche hitched to four gray horses. With him rode Mayor Bigelow, Judge Cleaver of the Common Council and Attorney General Dayton; from all the President-Elect elicited promises that there would be no introductions, handshakings or speeches.

One reporter declared that "it seemed as though [the] entire population of half the state had gone wild with enthusiasm and delight" at the sight of Mr. Lincoln and, this journalist declared, "the roofs of stores, dwellings, factories and sheds were covered with nearly as many spectators as were in the streets." Another reporter declared that "men, women and children were temporarily insane." Ladies scattered flowers and threw kisses as Mr. Lincoln passed, and, wrote the correspondent for the *Philadelphia Inquirer,* "stalwart mechanics cheered as though their lungs were made of bell metal." Some were trampled as thousands followed the barouche, and, declared a witness, "the esteem of the citizens appeared to amount to worship."

Mr. Lincoln admitted that he had not been received with such overwhelming affection since leaving Springfield, Illinois. Flags decorated store fronts. Students at the Ninth Ward Public School stood on three platforms decorated with "elegant" silk flags and serenaded the President-Elect with a chorus of "Hail Columbia" (although the *Inquirer* reporter believed that the melody was "We Are a Band of Brothers"). Mr. Lincoln rose in the carriage, removed his hat, and bowed three times to the children. One store embellished the scene with the effigy of a gibbeted slave-owner with whip in hand and titled this display "The Doom of Traitors." A Thomas Winton had his collarbone broken in the crush of the crowd, but decided that seeing the President-Elect justified this sacrifice.

As the barouche neared the Chestnut Street Station the throng of admirers grew so numerous that a body of horsemen had to open a lane so that Mr. Lincoln could reach the train. At about this time in the Trenton State House an Assemblyman offered the resolution "That when this house shall have seen Abraham Lincoln, they will have seen the ugliest man in the country." The resolution was tabled.

Snow began to fall by the time the Presidential train reached Elizabeth. A band played the "Star Spangled Banner," and Mr. Lincoln greeted the crowd from the rear platform of his personal car. At Rahway, where a special reception had been arranged at DeGraw's Hotel and a crowd of 3,000 had gathered, the train rushed by without stopping because Lincoln had begun to complain about his growing fatigue. Guns of welcome echoed from Rahway as the train swept on. About five thousand people awaited the President-Elect at New Brunswick, where engines had to be changed.

Among those who waited was John C. Van Dyke, then a
child, who watched the proceedings from "high up on the
box seat of an old family carriage." He could see over the
heads of the people and wondered "where all those people
lived and who made their hats." More than by the bands
that were playing and the flags that were flying young Van
Dyke was fascinated by the hats. "I had never seen so
many," he recalled, "and they seemed to surge and mill and
eddy about like blocks of wood in a whirlpool." *

The sound of the approaching train brought a cry: "Here
he comes." There was pushing on both sides of the track
and stern shouts from the constabulary to "Stand back,
there." Young Van Dyke remembered:

"An alley was formed through the crowd, and down that
alley came slowly gliding a short train of cars. They were
the dumpy little cars of the Camden and Amboy Railroad,
but to my eyes they appeared colossal. And how gay they
looked! The cars were streaming with red, white, and blue
flags and festoonings, the engine was wound about with
bright ribbons, and even the trainman, who sat up in his little 'buggy' cover on top of the engine, holding the bell rope
over the tops of the cars, had a flag wrapped around his hat.
There was a tremendous hurrah as the cars slowly drew
through the crowd and came to a stand-still. . . ."

But an even greater astonishment awaited young Van
Dyke, for when two men appeared on the platform the child
screamed loudly, "There's Father! There's Father!" Heads
turned angrily toward the source of this impudent interrup-
tion. Yet, indeed, it was Judge Van Dyke of the State Su-
preme Court who had been selected to welcome Lincoln to
New Brunswick. The child recalled: "a boy's father is always a big man to the boy. But that other man! What a

* John C. Van Dyke, "A Child's Impression of Lincoln," *A New Jersey
Reader* (New Brunswick, N.J., 1961), pp. 154–55.

giant he must be, I thought, for he was so much taller! He was dressed in long black clothes, had long arms and legs, a long face, and on his head a long silk hat. I couldn't help looking at him. He seemed such a very odd-looking man as he stood there taking off his hat occasionally by way of bowing to periodic bursts of applause. He was there for only a few moments, and then the train moved off amid great shouts."

At Princeton the students greeted the President-Elect with an "ear-splitting, sky-rocketing cheer" and Mr. Lincoln bowed to them from the "hinder platform." Almost to a man the Princetonians boarded the excursion train that followed the Lincoln Special and thus "pursued" the President-Elect with merry bursts of song.

Lincoln finally reached Trenton at 11:50. Sunshine splashed over the city, increasing the holiday spirit of spectators who had come from Belvidere, Burlington, Lambertville, from Easton, Pennsylvania, and smaller communities too numerous to name. It was a great day for the pickpockets, who, by the estimate of the local police, cleared a good $5,000 before the festivities ended.

The President-Elect agreed to address briefly both branches of the New Jersey Legislature. In the Senate he recalled his feelings when as a boy he had read Parson Weems's *Life of Washington:*

". . . I remember all the accounts there given of the battle fields and struggles for the liberties of the country, and none fix themselves upon my imagination as deeply as the struggle here at Trenton, New-Jersey. The crossing of the river; the contest with the Hessians; the great hardships endured at that time, all fix themselves on my memory more than any single Revolutionary event; and you all know, for you have all been boys, how these early impressions last longer than any others. I recollect thinking then, boy even though I was, that there must have been something more than common that those men struggled for. . . ." *

Lincoln was escorted from the upper chamber by a senator with the remarkable name of Reckless, and introduced to the Speaker of the General Assembly, whose equally remarkable name was Teese. "I shall do all that may be in my power to promote a peaceful settlement of our difficulties," Mr. Lincoln told the assemblymen. "The man does not live who is more devoted to peace than I am. None who would do more to preserve it. But it may be necessary to put the foot down firmly." From the Capitol, Mr. Lincoln went to the Trenton House and from a staging erected at one of the windows bowed to the military companies and the great crowd of people who had come to show their support of him as their next President. Shortly after 2 P.M. Mr. Lincoln's train rattled over the bridge across the Delaware.

Seven weeks and one day later the Confederates fired on Fort Sumter and the Civil War began.

For the thousandth and final time the author denies that President Lincoln ever visited Cape May or hunted birds in the marshes of Secaucus. Yet the circumstances of a second visit by the President on June 25, 1862, were exceptional. Mr. Lincoln had come north to discuss military matters with General Winfield Scott, who was then director of West Point. At 11:00 on Wednesday morning, June 25, General Scott accompanied the President to the ferry depot at Jersey City. Lincoln's other escorts were Colonel Daniel Craig McCallum, military director of railroads, and a Negro servant. About thirty people gathered for an impromptu

---

* Historian Emeritus Mearns doubts the authenticity of these remarks, believing that Lincoln was too tired to speak this clearly, and substitutes a meandering, meaningless passage that appeared in the *Trenton Daily State Gazette and Republican* (*Largely Lincoln*, p. 77); but Dr. Basler includes the story in the *Collected Works*, IV, 235–36, basing his source upon the report in the *New York Tribune* for the following day, February 22, 1861.

welcome and remarked on how well the President looked. Mr. Lincoln assured the people that no special national emergency had taken him to the interview with General Scott. He reminded his audience of the tight restrictions imposed on the press by Secretary of War Edward M. Stanton and excused himself from saying more by adding that "if I should blab anything they cannot publish, I do not know what he will do with me." The President boarded a special two-car train and, according to the *Washington Star,* set a new record for the run between New York and the capital. That evening with several friends, including Senator Orville H. Browning of Illinois, Lincoln visited the Soldiers' Home.

Next morning the Seven Days' Battle to take Richmond began.

As the war neared the close of its second year, the New Jersey Legislature acted with incredible political impudence. The "Peace" Democrats and Copperheads, if any distinction existed between these two groups, were especially inflamed by the Emancipation Proclamation that asked Jerseymen to risk their lives in order to free the "nigger." In the passage of "Peace Resolutions" on March 18, 1863, New Jersey was asked to withdraw its fighting men from the Union Army and the opponents of the war enumerated against the Lincoln Administration a list of specific protests:

"Against a war waged with the insurgent States for the accomplishment of unconstitutional or partisan purposes;

"Against a war which has for its object the subjugation of any of the States, with a view to their reduction to territorial condition;

"Against proclamations from any source by which, under the plea of 'military necessity,' persons in States and Territories sustaining the Federal Government, and beyond necessary military lines, are held liable to the rigor and severity of military laws;

"*Against* the domination of the military over the civil law in States, Territories, or districts not in a state of insurrection;

"*Against* all arrests without warrant; against the suspension of the writ of *habeas corpus* in States and Territories sustaining the Federal Government, 'where the public safety does not require it,' and against the assumption of power by any person to suspend such writ, except under the express authority of Congress;   .

"*Against* the creation of new States by the division of existing ones, or in any other manner not clearly authorized by the Constitution, and against the right of secession as practically admitted by the action of Congress in admitting as a new State a portion of the State of Virginia [West Virginia];

"*Against* the power assumed in the proclamation of the President made January first, 1863, by which all the slaves in certain States and parts of States are for ever set free; and against the expenditures of the public moneys for the emancipation of slaves or their support at any time, under any pretence whatever;

"*Against* any and every exercise of power upon the part of the Federal Government that is not clearly given and expressed in the Federal Constitution—reasserting that 'the powers not delegated to the United States by the Constitution, nor prohibited by it to the States, are reserved to the States respectively, or to the people.'"

For these reasons the hostile legislators called upon New Jersey to appoint commissioners to meet with similar representatives of other insurgent states to convene for the purpose of devising a plan, "consistent with the honor and dignity of the national government," for securing a peace "under the blessing of God." *

* Frank Moore, ed., *The Rebellion Record: A Diary of American Events* (New York, 1861–1868), XII, 679–81.

Twenty-eight officers of the 11th New Jersey, camped below Falmouth, Virginia, retorted with indignation. As members of a state "hallowed by the remembrance of the battles of Princeton, Trenton, and Monmouth," these officers scorned a legislature that would "tarnish" the State's high honor by resolutions calling for a "dishonorable peace." The soldiers in the field, these New Jersey officers declared, were willing "to endure the fatigues, privations, and dangers incident to a soldier's life in order to maintain our Republic in its integrity," even if this duty involved the sacrifice of their lives. Grimly they resolved: "That we regard as traitors alike the foe in arms and the secret enemies of our Government, who, at home, foment disaffection and strive to destroy confidence in our legally chosen rulers."

The rabidly anti-Lincoln newspapers joined in the dispute. The *Monmouth Democrat* of Freehold sneered when Lincoln's oldest son, Robert, joined his mother at a vacation resort in the White Mountains and wondered why he was not risking his life for the freedom of the Negro. After the victory at Gettysburg the equally anti-Lincoln *New Brunswick Times* reported: "certain office-holders—some of them selected by Democratic votes—labored hard all day to do *something,* and that night a procession was formed and marched through our streets. Cannon were fired, rockets were set off, tar barrels were burnt, and cheers were given at the houses of the most prominent Abolitionists. Insulting remarks were freely indulged in, in meeting or passing the houses of men who support the Union, the Constitution, and the Laws, and don't just think the nigger is better than the white men." *

The anti-Lincoln politicians and newspapers had misread the spirit of the people, so well expressed by Commodore Richard F. Stockton, who each morning hoisted "the Star

* Earl Schenck Miers, *New Jersey and the Civil War* (Princeton, N.J., 1964), pp. 109–11.

Spangled Banner at Morven, the former residence of one
of the signers of the Declaration of Independence." The
Commodore alluded to his grandfather, who had built
Morven. The Commodore had himself been a naval hero
in the War of 1812 and many were certain to listen when
he declared that the present crisis justified any sacrifice a
Jerseyman could make.

On a hot and sticky August morning my wife and I found
Finn's Point. We drove south through Pennsville on Route
49 and turned west onto the road to Fort Mott. The day
was breathless and we had a feeling of going back through
time to that pre-Revolutionary age when the Swedes and
Finns and Quakers dreamed of turning this small part of
West Jersey into a personal paradise. The houses were few,
and the smaller homes appeared deserted. Beside the road
the tasseled marsh reeds had grown to a height higher than
our heads.

Finn's Point National Cemetery, no larger than four and
a half acres, is probably the northernmost burial ground for
Confederate soldiers supported by the national government.
During the Civil War, Pea Patch Island in the Delaware
River, about a mile and a half from Finn's Point, was a
Union prison whose population was increased rapidly by
Confederate prisoners captured at the Battle of Gettysburg.
The smallness of the island, particularly at periods of high
water, rendered the area unsuitable for the burial of the
dead, so the Finn's Point National Cemetery was created
on part of the land which the United States had purchased
in 1837 to establish a battery for the protection of the Port
of Philadelphia.

A stout man in overalls was seated on a power mower
when we stopped at the director's office at Finn's Point. The
office itself was deserted although there were stacks of material concerning the installation of the fort and cemetery.

We were helping ourselves to these leaflets when the man who had been mowing appeared. He was the director.

"I always figure the public will snoop around and find what it wants whether or not I'm here," he said. "But that's all right with me—anything valuable I keep locked in the desk."

I introduced myself and explained that I wrote books.

"Never read 'em," he said.

"Oh, come," I teased, "I bet you peek into a pornographic novel now and then."

"Wouldn't tell you if I did." But he grinned. "Well," he said, "I think I'll get back to my mowing. There's nothing nicer in the world than the smell of fresh-cut grass."

No director could have fitted more perfectly into the traditions of Finn's Point, where, in all, 2,436 members of the Confederacy are buried in six trenches. One hundred and thirty-five Union soldiers who died guarding the prisoners on Pea Patch Island occupy three trenches.

The Finn's Point National Cemetery was established in 1875 and its first superintendent was Frederick Schmidt, a Union soldier who had lost an arm during the war. His salary was $60 a month, and $8.50 of this sum paid for the lodge he rented at Salem, New Jersey, about a six-mile jog on horseback. Schmidt was determined that the cemetery should not be the mud hole he found. He seeded the ground and planted trees at the prices they brought in 1876. Seventy-five cents purchased a Norway maple and a silver maple could be bought for fifty cents. A Norway pine from three to six feet in height also was worth half a dollar. Schmidt's progress so attracted his superiors in Washington that he was made superintendent of the National Cemetery at Baton Rouge, Louisiana.

The next supervisor at Finn's Point was Charles F. Eichwurzel, an old Indian fighter in Nebraska and Wyoming. Memorial Day services at Finn's Point were elaborate occasions in the 1880's. People lined both sides of the road with their buggies, phaetons and barouches. Flowers covered the graves and bands played lively martial tunes. Some came to the ceremonies on excursion steamers, but an ominous note crept into the report for 1882: "Seven men were 'rejected' for misbehaving." The offenders, who had brought a keg of beer, moved down the road about fifty yards from the cemetery, where they "commenced to drink, curse and make annoyance." An enraged Eichwurzel "dispersed the gang," but admitted afterward that he had acted illegally, for his authority extended to only eight feet on any side of the cemetery.

In 1879 the United States erected a marble monument to the memory of the 105 Union soldiers who still could be identified. In 1910 an obelisk eighty-five feet high, a structure of reinforced concrete faced with Pennsylvania white granite, contained on bronze plates the names of the 2,436 Confederate prisoners interred here. The period was one of deep sentimentalism, and on seven bronze tablets, each set on its own mounting, the following verses appeared:

> The muffled drums sad roll has beat
> The soldier's last tattoo.
> No more on life's parade shall meet
> That brave and fallen few.
>
> Your own proud land's heroic soil
> Must be your fitter grave;
> She claims from war his richest spoil,
> The ashes of the grave.
>
> No rumor of the foe's advance
> Now sweeps upon the wind,
> No troubled thought at midnight haunts
> Of loved ones left behind.

No vision of the morrow's strife
The warrior's dream alarms.
No braying horn nor screaming fife
At dawn shall call to arms.

The neighing troop, the flashing blade,
The bugle's stirring blast.
The charge, the dreadful cannonade,
The din and shout are past.

On fame's eternal camping-ground
Their silent tents are spread,
And glory guards with solemn round
The bivouac of the dead.

Rest on embalmed and sainted dead.
Dear as the blood ye gave.
No impious footstep here shall tread
The herbage of your grave.

Also buried at Finn's Point are veterans of the Spanish American War and World War I, who served at the fort when it was an active military installation. In one corner are the graves of thirteen German prisoners of World War II who died while in captivity at Fort Dix. The government intends that there shall be no further burials at Finn's Point.

It was not until 1897 that the fort was named to honor General Gershom Mott, commander of New Jersey Volunteers during the Civil War. Mott was born at Lamberton (now part of Trenton) on April 7, 1822. He attended Trenton Academy until he was fourteen years of age, when he became a clerk in a dry-goods store. Later he served without distinction during the Mexican War as a Second Lieutenant with the Tenth United States Infantry. Afterward he became collector of the port at Lamberton, then was appointed to a responsible position with the Bordentown, Delaware & Raritan Canal Company. He was teller of the Bordentown Banking Company when the Civil War began.* Mott served brilliantly with the Army of the Potomac from the Seven Days' Battle to the conquest of Petersburg and Richmond.

So, despite the antics of its Peace Democrats, New Jersey gave distinguished service to the nation during the tragic years of rebellion. It was asked to enlist 78,248 troops and supplied 88,305. It paid $2,275,989 to dependents and $23,000,000 in bounties. Special hospitals for the wounded were established at Newark and Jersey City. In 1864 Princeton bestowed upon Lincoln *in absentia* the honorary degree of Doctor of Laws.

One morning the Van Dyke boy who had caused a disturbance when Lincoln stopped at New Brunswick en route to Washington in 1861 found his father holding the back of a chair and looking grave and sad. "In a choking voice" the Judge spoke to his son:

"What do you think—they have shot the tall man, they have killed Mr. Lincoln."

The boy remembered the tears in the steel-gray eyes as his father spoke.

Through "my own tears of childish sympathy" the boy looked up and asked: "Did the tall man have to die to save us?"

"It seems so—it seems so," his father said.

On April 24, 1865, Lincoln paid his last visit to New Jersey. Even in farm areas the people came down to the trackside to honor the funeral train of the martyred President. Sober-faced men stood with their hats pressed against their hearts, farm women wiped the mist from their eyes with

---

* Donovan Yeuell, sketch of Mott, *Dictionary of American Biography.*

their aprons, and the children gathered wild flowers from the meadows and strewed them upon the tracks before the train appeared. A sign in the depot at Jersey City told well what was in the hearts of Jerseymen that day:

GEORGE WASHINGTON THE FATHER
ABRAHAM LINCOLN THE SAVIOR,
OF OUR COUNTRY.

9

The Wonderful Wizard of . . .

By 1909 seven new states had been admitted to the Union so that Walter C. Letson, the final orator for his class, wore a sash of forty-six stars. Many changes had taken place. Raritan [Edison] Township had been formed out of part of Piscataway and Woodbridge townships, a spire had been put on the church, and Baptist Roads had become Stelton "with a post offis and four mails a day." Trains sped by at the rate of a mile a minute. "At Menlo Park," Master Letson continued, "Mr. Edison built the first trolley car, and in 1880 or '81, it made its trial trip over a track laid for the purpose from Menlo Park to Oak Tree. Trolley cars, bicycles, electric lights, electric motors, electric bells, telefones, fonografs, automobiles, and wireless telegrafy have all come into use during this period."

In an age when science had begun to change the way of life in America, New Jersey supplied its full share of wizards. Certainly Thomas Edison was a legitimate candidate for leader of this group, but there were others. The situation was somewhat like a joke some adults might ask to confuse a child: If on going to sleep you counted sheep and suddenly visualized an extraordinary animal with three heads, did you

106

count it as three sheep or one? In the same spirit, New Jersey could ask where its most wonderful wizard of science had lived. Perth Amboy? Menlo Park? Trenton? Atlantic City?

Early in the nineteenth century an inventive genius named Solomon Andrews was born in Perth Amboy. At seventeen it was not the sermons of his father as pastor of the Presbyterian Church that held the boy's rapt attention, but the sight through an open window of an eagle soaring in flight. Watching the bird's movement, Solomon wrote, all at once he sat erect as though experiencing "an electric shock." * Henceforth Solomon was obsessed by the dream of someday constructing an aircraft permitting a man to soar through the air like the eagle.

Young Andrews studied medicine and worked as a watchmaker; as a result of his inventive mind he secured patents for a barrel-making machine, a sewing machine, fumigators, forging presses, velocipedes, gas lamps, a padlock for mailbags and a kitchen stove. He took over the barracks that the British had used when they held Perth Amboy during the Revolution and converted these structures into "The Inventor's Institute." His was the conception of a kind of phalanx for scientists, which he advertised in newspapers of 1850. There were seven buildings arranged in "a hollow square." They included a keg factory, an engine house, a machine shop, a United States mail padlock factory, an office, and a wing "divided into eight distinct apartments for private workshops of inventors."

Solomon erected a structure looking somewhat like "a ship house" in which to build his first airship. He devised a

---

* Solomon Andrews, *The Art of Flying* (New York, 1865), an extremely rare book, of which the only extant copy known is in the library of the Department of Defense; see also Earl Schenck Miers, *Where the Raritan Flows* (New Brunswick, N.J., 1964), pp. 71ff.

wooden framework eighty feet long, twenty feet wide and
ten feet in depth. Thirteen thousand yards of silk, woven
in China, covered this framework and was inflated with hydrogen. Confidently Andrews advertised his airship in New
York newspapers, saying that the aircraft could be seen at
The Inventor's Institute on July 4, 1850, and told his readers that "the plan of the invention was laid 23 years since
and has occupied the attention of its projector during that
period." Tickets at fifty cents each would admit "a gentleman and a lady" to the exhibit and demonstration and "every
additional lady" would be admitted for twenty-five cents. A
crowd gathered to see Solomon's masterpiece, but poor
Andrews had to confess his failure: "The vessel was never
taken out of the house. A small machine, about 12′ long, was
filled and let go to the upper regions. It was sent toward the
sea, and never afterwards heard from."

Solomon remained undaunted by his numerous scoffers.
With the coming of the Civil War his mind was inflamed
with the idea of how the proper aircraft could shorten that
struggle and save the Union. He wrote directly to President
Lincoln, saying, in part:

"The plan is so simple that the cost will not be much more
than that of a common balloon, but it will require secrecy
to prevent the enemy from becoming acquainted therewith
before our Government shall have received its benefits.
I have no doubt of being able to give it locomotion in any
and every direction, not only in calm weather, but against a
considerable wind. As the best evidence of my confidence in
the project, permit me to say that I am willing to pledge
real estate now in my possession, valued at not less than fifty
thousand dollars, for the success of the undertaking. I will
sail the air ship, when constructed, five to ten miles into
Secessia and back again, or no pay."

President Lincoln did not reply. An impatient Solomon
wrote to Secretary of War Edwin Stanton and was an-

swered by P. H. Watson, the Assistant Secretary, who told Solomon that if he would send drawings and descriptions of the aircraft they would be referred to the Chief of Ordnance, "who will advise you if your invention is found to possess anything new and of practical utility, adapted to and needed for the public service."

Solomon departed at once for Washington to submit his drawings and a description of the invention to the War Department. The Bureau of Topographical Engineers examined the project thoroughly while Solomon paced the floor for three days. He was asked how much the airship would cost and replied that the expense would not exceed $5,000, "and I would guarantee its success, or no pay." Next a Major Woodruff queried Solomon as to what constituted his motive power and seemed stunned when Andrews, cautiously secretive about details, replied: "Gravitation." He returned to Perth Amboy and awaited the decision. A week later Solomon heard from Assistant Secretary P. H. Watson, who confessed that the Bureau of Topographical Engineers had found his aerostat a "device" that appeared "to be ingenious in a high degree," but that they could not conceive of his method of locomotion and therefore could not judge the invention of having "practical utility." Solomon wrote snappishly to Secretary of War Stanton because the drawings and description of the aircraft had not been returned, adding testily that "I intend to build one immediately on my own account, and if successful I shall present it to the U.S. Government, in the hope that it may shorten the war."

Solomon commenced immediately to build the ship. He purchased 1,300 yards of cambric muslin, which was varnished, and hired a carpenter to build him fifteen spheres twelve feet in diameter and six seven feet in diameter. The spheres came out looking like balloons, and a disgruntled Solomon had to start anew. This time he purchased about

1,200 yards of Irish linen, which was varnished and used to cover three cylindroids. The machine was filled with eleven 200-gallon hogsheads of hydrogen. Fourteen of the spheroidal balloons formerly constructed were inflated inside of the two outer cylindroids "to divide them into compartments for safety, and for other reasons." The first trial made in June, 1863, proved a failure when the balloons leaked and collapsed, whereas the other cylindroids remained intact and firm. Andrews redesigned his aircraft on the basis of these experiences and, he wrote President Lincoln, would be "ready for the final trial on August 26."

The reporter for the *New York Herald* was so impressed by the success of Andrews' ship in flight that the journalist called it "the most extraordinary invention of the age, if not the most so of any the world ever saw." The *Herald,* a viciously anti-Lincoln newspaper, ribbed the Secretary of War for his failure to see the utility "of a machine which could go over into Secesh and reconnoitre the force and position of the enemy." Indeed, the newspaper did not hesitate to label those who had rejected the original plans as "stupid." Upon three occasions reporters from the *Herald* accompanied Andrews on trial flights and described the nature of the ship:

"Its form was that of three cigars pointed at both ends, secured together at their longitudinal equator, covered by a net, and supporting by one hundred and twenty cords a [wicker] car sixteen feet below, under its centre."

The *Herald* reporter described how Solomon's dirigible-like flying ship operated:

". . . he set her off in a spiral course upward, she going at a rate of not less than one hundred and twenty miles per hour, and describing circles in the air of more than one and a half miles in circumference. . . . She passed through the first strata of dense white clouds, about two miles high, scattering them as she entered in all directions. In her upward flight could be distinctly seen her rapid movement in a contrary direction to the moving clouds, and as she came before the wind passing by them with great celerity . . . with the sun shining clear upon her, there could be no mistake or optical delusion to the beholder."

Solomon, understanding how his craft could be used for reconnaissance and even for dropping bombs on Southern cities, prepared for a new hassle with the authorities at Washington by petitioning the Senate and the House of Representatives. He wrote disgustedly: "The petition to the House could not be found one week after its presentation." Letters between Perth Amboy and the chairman of the military committee of the House passed like poison darts. Finally, the chairman, Robert C. Schenck, returned the drawings and other material without referring the invention to the consideration of Congress.

Solomon, cheered by the end of the war, proposed next to demonstrate his aircraft's great value "for commercial purposes" and "for the benefit of mankind." On June 6, 1866, he made a run from Perth Amboy to Oyster Bay on Long Island. This time the *New York Times* described the astonishment of promenaders on Broadway as they beheld "a large fish sailing in the air about 1500 feet over their heads." The street became chaotic as the spectators walked along with heads thrown back. "The fair sex," the *Times* reported, "seemed to become oblivious of the presence of the fashionable swells, and in their abstraction ran their sunshades into their eyes; while the gentlemen equally absent-minded played sad havoc with the hoops and other appendages of the perambulating milliners' frames." The balloon, said the *New York Post*, "kept her course before the wind, the aeronauts throwing out sand, which being very dry could be seen in little clouds." Among the onlookers Solomon also scattered leaflets reading: "Souvenir of her trial trip from the car of Andrews' Flying Ship."

But for all the curiosity he aroused Solomon could not find financial backing to organize the Aerial Navigation Company, which was intended to operate aircraft for carrying passengers and mail between cities and towns. He was three times mayor of Perth Amboy, frequently a member of the city council, and Health Officer of the Port, but died in October, 1872, a sad man who had not fulfilled his dream.

Today when jet airliners pass over our home they already have entered the landing pattern that will carry them in a few minutes to Newark Airport. We watch them and remember Solomon Andrews.

When Thomas Alva Edison, then in his early thirties, came to Menlo Park in 1876, this country village consisted of about a half-dozen dwellings.* The hamlet was only twenty-five miles by railroad from New York City, where Edison solicited much of his work. Soon hammers banged and saws buzzed. First to be constructed was Edison's main laboratory, a two-story building thirty feet wide and a hundred feet long. Then a machine shop was erected, followed by a glass-blowers' shed. Another small structure was called the carbon shed, for there Edison produced the lamp-black carbon he finally used in the filament for his incandescent light. An office building and library, where an exhausted Edison often slept on the desk top, completed the group of buildings not unlike Solomon Andrews' one-time Inventor's Institute.

Edison was a pragmatist who believed in working on no invention that did not promise use by the public. He also was a thrifty man who believed in wasting nothing, and so by opening an old copper mine in Mine Gully, a mile north of Menlo Park, he secured the ore for making the tracks on

* Earl Schenck Miers, *Where the Raritan Flows* (New Brunswick, N.J., 1964), pp. 106ff.

which his electric railroad ran. For the Western Union Company he perfected the telephone, and among his other inventions was the phonograph, which started a craze he had not anticipated. Edison was invited by President Rutherford B. Hayes to bring his phonograph to the White House, and the pair discussed the invention until three o'clock in the morning. By carriage and train hundreds of visitors came to inspect "the village of science," and rare was the scientist from overseas who neglected a pilgrimage to Menlo Park.

The Eternal Light that now burns at Menlo Park is the symbol of Edison's greatest accomplishment. Edison worked for two years before he perfected this invention. In his search for a long-burning filament, he tested more than ten thousand different substances, from platinum to bright red hair plucked from the beard of a friend. But at last he found his answer—carbonized cotton thread—which burned steadily for forty hours.

Edison's light, called the sensation of the age, was used to welcome the New Year of 1880. Three thousand visitors jammed around Menlo Park and cheered wildly when at midnight a dozen lights were turned on. Later Edison performed a more sensational demonstration by wiring six houses and the surrounding fields and roads with 450 lights. Darkness closed in. Curious onlookers waited in almost breathless silence. Edison flicked the switch and like magic Menlo Park burst into light.

Spectators paid to ride in his small railroad or "trolley," and a little engine run by a dynamo in the laboratory generating system pulled the curious through the woods toward Pumptown and the water tank which stood near Dismal Swamp at Metuchen.

Edison was called to assignments throughout the country. His family enjoyed the gently rolling hills around Menlo Park, especially during summer months, but after Mrs.

Edison died from typhoid fever in 1884, her husband
moved to West Orange and never again visited the village.
The laboratory at Menlo Park was converted into a cow
barn and might have been lost forever had not Henry Ford
bought the structure for his Museum of Industry and Invention at Dearborn, Michigan. Ford also reopened the
shaft in Mine Gully, but the copper was all gone. Still,
Ford bought carloads of Menlo Park dirt to haul to Michigan, thereby transporting the Japanese beetle to another
environment. At Dearborn in the reconstructed laboratory
from Menlo Park, Ford observed the fiftieth anniversary of
the discovery of the incandescent light. Among the visitors
to Dearborn that day was Thomas Alva Edison, then in his
eighties.

The Roeblings of Trenton were tenacious in their loves
and hatreds and in their passion for hard work that produced new wonders of the world. The family had reached
New Jersey by a circuitous route. John A. Roebling, the
sire of the American branch of the clan, was born June 12,
1806, in Mühlhausen, Thuringia, the youngest son of a
father noted as a tobacco manufacturer. The German Roeblings were people of modest means, and it was only through
his mother's self-denial and thrift that John was enabled
to attend the Royal Polytechnic Institute in Berlin. Among
his teachers was the great philosopher Hegel, whom John
virtually worshipped and from whom he may have obtained
his life-long opposition to human slavery in any form. He
worked as a road-builder and then as a constructor of a
chain-suspension bridge at Bamberg in Bavaria.

Like many Germans of his time John Roebling dreamed
of emigrating to America and in 1831 settled in Pennsylvania at Saxonburg, where he became a farmer. He was
accompanied by his brother Karl, and together they bought
7,000 acres of land in Butler County, approximately twenty-

five miles from Pittsburgh. He married in Saxonburg in 1834, his first successful venture in America, for he certainly was not qualified to be an agriculturalist.

Washington Augustus Roebling, the first of John's nine children, was born May 26, 1837, and as he grew to young manhood he laughed when he recalled his father's mounting frustration in this "wild land" as he tried to "dig and delve" for an existence in the hard clay of Butler County. Under the land where John struggled was the great Golden Eagle well that eventually spouted 3,000 barrels of oil a day, but Wash shrugged his shoulders when he confessed that his father had refused an interest in the original Rockefeller syndicate. "So," Wash said of his father, "he put all his money in shale and lost every cent he put in, but at the same time escaped being a second Rockefeller. Thank God! What would I have done with a billion of dollars?" *

John Roebling returned to engineering, the profession for which he was trained. Canals were a major enterprise of this era, and John worked for the Allegheny Portage Railroad, an important link between eastern and western Pennsylvania. The canal boats there were placed on cars to be pulled by the railway over steep inclines, and to Roebling the cables used for hauling the cars were poorly constructed. These hawsers, usually about three inches thick, were made of Kentucky hemp and broke frequently. It was then that John Roebling insured the fame of Wash and himself by conceiving the idea of constructing the cables from twisted wires. John began manufacturing wire rope in a small factory in Saxonburg, but, since the demand for the material expanded rapidly, he needed a more convenient location and in 1848 or 1849 moved to Trenton.

* Sketches of John and Washington Roebling, *Dictionary of American Biography;* William C. Conant, "The Brooklyn Bridge," *Harper's New Monthly Magazine* (May, 1883), pp. 925ff.; Washington Augustus Roebling Papers, mss., Rutgers University Library.

It was during this period that Wash attended Trenton Academy and then Rensselaer Polytechnic Institute, "that terrible treadmill of forcing an avalanche of figures and facts into young brains not qualified to assimilate them as yet." Even then Wash was acquiring his reputation as an "oddball" who possessed no restraint in voicing his opinions of those around him. He worked in his father's wire-rope mill and then assisted his father in building the Allegheny River bridge at Pittsburgh, which was completed in the summer of 1860. Father and son returned to Trenton the summer preceding the Civil War, and when that tragic event occurred, John, still holding to his hatred for human slavery, insisted that Wash join the Union army.

Wash quickly became an engineer with the Army of the Potomac, a military organization so big that when it moved it was like a town vanishing with all its stores, houses, people, horses and mules, wagons, livestock, weapons, hospitals and other equipment. Yet even within this massive fighting force Wash retained his individuality. A contemporary described him:

"R. is a character, a major and aide-de-camp and engineer, and factotum to General Warren. He is a son of the German engineer, Roebling, who built the celebrated suspension bridge over the Niagara River [1851–55]. He is a light-haired, blue-eyed man, with a countenance as if all the world were an empty show. He stoops a great deal, when riding his stirrups so long that the tips of his toes can just touch them, and, as he wears no boots, the bottoms of his pantaloons are always torn and ragged. He goes poking about in the most dangerous places, looking for the position of the enemy, and always with an air of entire indifference. His conversation is curt and not garnished with polite trimmings. 'What's that redoubt doing there?' cries General Meade. 'Don't know; didn't put it there,' replies the laconic one. The Chief [Meade] growled a little while at the earth-work, but, as that didn't move it, he rode onward." *

Wash was unusually loyal to General Gouverneur K. Warren, and insisted that Warren alone had saved Little Round Top, the pivotal point of victory for the Union at Gettysburg. When Grant went east to lead the Army of the Potomac in its final campaign against Lee and seemed to slight Warren, Wash referred to the mid-Westerner as "Useless" Grant. The fact that young Roebling was in love with Miss Emily Warren, the sister of General Warren, may have colored his judgment. In love Wash verged on the brink of goofiness. His early love letters started quite reasonably with "Dear Emmie" but as the affair advanced his salutations included "My lazy Darling," "Sweet Angel of Purity," and "My dear Sister in the Lord."

By the close of the war John A. Roebling was already engaged in what would become his most spectacular achievement. One winter too many of suffering the discomforts of ferrying across the East River to work in Manhattan had convinced Brooklynites that a bridge must span this river. The original cost was estimated at five million dollars, and Brooklyn, which remained an independent city until 1898, agreed to pay two-thirds of this sum. Naturally, when everybody had their ideas incorporated into the plans the cost increased to thrice this amount. Army engineers, for example, wanted the bridge raised five feet above the origi-nal height so that the tallest masted schooner could pass under it.

On a summer day in 1869, John Roebling rested his foot on a piling as he studied the possible location of the tower on the Brooklyn side of the river. A ferryboat entered the slip and struck the pilings in a manner to catch and crush

---

* George R. Aggassiz, ed., *Meade's Headquarters, 1863–1865, Letters of Colonel Theodore Lyman from the Wilderness to Appomattox* (Boston, 1922), p. 240.

his foot. Several toes were amputated and within sixteen days John Roebling was dead of lockjaw. He did not see the first stone laid in his magnificent enterprise.

Wash was expected to complete the bridge. Among other difficulties it was discovered that the air-compressed chambers which the men used in digging to the bedrock on which the foundations must rest had to penetrate seventy-five feet of mud. No one had ever worked at such a depth, and the men often were stricken by "caisson disease" or the bends, a malady that produces an excess of oxygen and nitrogen within various bodily fluids. After too rapid decompression a worker could be afflicted with severe pains. Cases are known where the pains and blood clots combined to cause prostration and death. Wash himself was laid up in 1872 with "caisson disease." Over a span of ten years he carried on his administrative work from his bedside. William C. Conant described in *Harper's New Monthly Magazine* for May the wonder of a celebration that the tenacious Wash could not attend:

"The summer of 1883 will be memorable for the opening of the great bridge, uniting New York and Brooklyn into a metropolis of nearly two million people—a population that will soon outgrow Paris, and have only London left to vie with. The bridge is practically a new street, belonging jointly to the two cities, and making with Third Avenue, the Bowery, and Chatham Street, New York, and Fulton Street continuing into Fulton Avenue on the Brooklyn side, a great thoroughfare fourteen miles long, already continuously built up, from the Harlem River to East New York. This is longer than the great street which stretches east to west across London, under its various names, from Bow to Uxbridge Road, spanning the valley, where was once the Fleet brook, by that other fine work of engineering, the Holborn Viaduct. The bridge roadway from its New York terminus opposite the City Hall to Sands Street,

Brooklyn, is a little over a mile long (5989 feet), and it
will take the pace of a smart walker to make the aerial
journey, with its arched ascent, in twenty minutes. The cities
will probably decide, confining the tolls to vehicular traffic,
not to charge him the one cent first proposed for the privi-
lege of taking this trip on 'foot's horse.' But for five cents
he can jump at either end into fine cars, built on the pattern
of the newest Manhattan elevated cars, which move apparently of their own volition, until one finds the secret in the
endless wire rope underneath that is worked by stationary
engines on the shore and makes continual circuit, across
under one roadway and back under the other. These will
take him across in a little less than five minutes, and it is not
improbable that through trains will ultimately convey passengers from the northernmost end of New York over the
Brooklyn Elevated that is to be, bringing them nearer to
the health-giving beaches of Long Island by nearly half an
hour's time.

"But the wise man will not cross the bridge in five minutes, nor in twenty. He will linger to get the good of the
splendid sweep of view about him, which his aesthetic self
will admit pays wonderful interest on his investment of
nothing. The bridge itself will be a remarkable sight, as he
looks from his central path of vantage down upon the
broad outer roadways, each with its tide of weighted
wagons and carriages of his wealthier but not wiser brethren, and nearer the centre the two iron paths upon which
the trains move silently and swiftly. Under him is the busy
river, the two great cities now made one, and beyond,
completing the circuit, villa-dotted Staten Island; the
marshes, rivers, and cities of New Jersey stretching to
Orange Mountain and the further heights; the Palisades
walling the mighty Hudson; the fair Westchester country;
the thoroughfare of the Sound opening out from Hell Gate;
Long Island, 'fish-shaped Paumanok,' with its beaches, the

Narrows, with their frowning forts; the Bay, where the
colossal Liberty will rise; at last the ocean, with its bridging
ships. And when he takes his walks about New York he
can scarcely lose sight of what is now the great landmark
which characterizes and dominates the city as St. Peter's
from across the Campagna dominates Rome, and the Arc
de Triomphe the approach to Paris, and the Capitol on its
height our own Washington—the double-towered bridge,
whose massive masonry finds no parallel since the Pyramids.
Those huger masses were the work of brutal force, piling
stone upon stone. The wonder and the triumph of this work
of our own day is in the weaving of the aerial span that
carries such burden of usefulness, by human thought and
skill, from the delicate threads of wire that a child could
almost sever."

Chester A. Arthur, who succeeded to the Presidency following the assassination of Garfield, cut the ribbon that
opened the bridge to the public, and so for the second time
during his administration Arthur rubbed elbows with science for he installed in the White House its first tile bath-
room. The era belonged to Horatio Alger, Jr., whose books
described how poor boys rose from rags to riches—poor
boys like John and Washington Augustus Roebling.

Aside from the mosquito, which, breeding in the bilge
water of tankers and freighters, has succeeded in invading
all five continents, New Jersey's best known accomplishment, throughout the nation, and perhaps the world, is the
creation of Atlantic City and its boardwalk.* That thrifty
Quaker, Thomas Budd, who arrived from England in 1678
and planned to begin a settlement on the upper Mullica
River, complained bitterly that he must also purchase the

---

* The source of most of the details in this section is William McMahon,
So Young . . . So Gay! (Atlantic City, N.J., 1970); it is a journalist's story
written with skill and affection.

islands that went with the mainland even though the cost was only four cents an acre. The three islands were named Sand Hills and Inside Beach, facing on Great Egg Inlet, and Cedar Beach, facing on Absecon Inlet and the Atlantic Ocean.

The principal occupation of the area was salt-hay farming, and to Simon Lake of Pleasantville went the credit for placing tractor-like chains on his hay carts so that they easily moved through meadows and marshland. Young couples were soon rowing out to the islands for beach parties and for a game they called "rolling the dunes," in which a young man seized a young lady, carried her to the top of the dune and rolled her down the banks to the edge of the water. Sport like this was worth four cents an acre! Yet, according to our authority, Mr. McMahon, the recreation "was all quite proper" when one considered the bathing garb of the day: "full pantaloons, stockings, skirts, jackets, wide brimmed hats and sometimes even gloves."

In time these three islands would become Atlantic City, and as early as 1853 investors interested in creating a seashore resort began raising the money for the Camden and Atlantic Railroad to run a rail line from Camden to Absecon Beach. Soon the Legislature approved the incorporation of the islands into a seashore resort, but land at first did not go very rapidly, even though lots could be bought at six dollars each. But the promoters kept plugging at advertising their city, and by 1870 the population had grown to 1,043. The city had become ten times this size by 1885. Among the inducements for coming to the resort was a free haircut—done with horse clippers! A bridge allowed the railroad to cross directly to the island city, where a horse and buggy could be hired for fifty cents an evening.

Beautiful gardens were planted and hotel accommodations for a week cost ten dollars. Mules were substituted for horses since they were considered much gentler to handle.

In the spring of 1870 there were two inventive entrepreneurs who turned Atlantic City into an American mecca. They were Jacob Kein, who owned the Chester County House on South New York Avenue, and Alexander Boardman, a conductor on the Camden and Atlantic Railroad, who also owned the Ocean House, a hotel on the southeast corner of Connecticut and Pacific avenues. Boardman took the lead in addressing the city fathers: "our visitors are no longer satisfied with the rough facilities once offered them here. Today we must supply fine carpets, good furniture and other luxuries. These cost money. Our carpets and even stuffed chairs are being ruined by the sand tracked into our places. . . . Walking on the beach is a favorite pastime. We can't stop this. We do propose to give the beach strollers [and presumably the innocent dune rollers] a walkway of boards above the sand which we believe will overcome our sand problem."

The board walkway was dedicated on June 26, 1870, with a parade and "celebration in all principal hotels [lasting] until the small hours." The first boardwalk, although the name was not officially adopted until 1896, was constructed in sections of twelve feet so that it could be taken up and stored during the winter months. The boards themselves were nailed to crosswise joists two feet apart. The walkway rose only eighteen inches above the sand, and yet its instant popularity could not be denied. Visitors to the nation's centennial celebration in Philadelphia in 1876 were attracted by the clever advertising of the railroad, and that year the first Easter Parade was held. Shopkeepers on Atlantic Avenue complained bitterly that the boardwalk was ruining their businesses, but they had no option but to move their stores to the boardwalk as it was improved over the years. Swinging lanterns, mounted on wooden poles, illuminated the boardwalk until 1912, when 299 of Mr. Edison's incandescent lights replaced the lamps, and people called this innovation "the last word in ornamental street lighting." The lights were turned off between "seasons," for Atlantic City had not yet become a year-round attraction. In 1914 city commissioner J. B. Thompson declared: "To say the boardwalk is Atlantic City's greatest asset is obvious and trite. As far as the lure and prosperity of Atlantic City is concerned it might as well lose the sea as the boardwalk. Possibly it could survive the loss of the former more than the latter, for the delights and fascination of the great promenade are all its own to tens of thousands of visitors and the sea is but an added attraction."

Luxurious hotels fronted the boardwalk. Piers stretched out into the ocean, were destroyed by fire or hurricane, and built anew while the force of the waves made necessary the reconstruction of Atlantic City's famous Steel Pier. Nothing seemed so consistent about the resort as the fact that there was always something new to stir the nation's interest in it. Thus, while parents raved, Annette Kellerman popularized the one-piece, form-fitting bathing suit.

A mystique came to surround Atlantic City and to make it especially attractive to people in the worlds of music, theater, and other arts. Historically, perhaps, this mystique had its beginning in the Gay Nineties when Diamond Jim Brady and Lillian Russell made their summer headquarters at the Shelburne Hotel. Victor Herbert was a constant visitor, along with George M. Cohan, who one night, scraping through a trunk for a melody he had long ago discarded, wrote new words and gave to America "Over There," the nation's rallying tune for World War I. Any number of personalities were likely to be seen strolling on the boardwalk: W. C. Fields, Jack Dempsey, Tom Mix, Douglas Fairbanks, Mary Pickford, Philip Sousa, Lawrence Tibbett, Galli-Curci, Enrico Caruso and a host of other stars of the stage, opera and silent screen. For a long period of time practically every show that succeeded in New York had a favorable tryout here, so that the shortest distance to Broadway was via the Atlantic City boardwalk.

The arrival of President Ulysses S. Grant in July, 1874, was cause for declaring a city holiday. Other Presidents who stayed in the city were William Howard Taft, Woodrow Wilson and Franklin D. Roosevelt. Convention Hall added to the attraction of the city, and it was here, of course, that Lyndon B. Johnson was nominated for the Presidency in 1964.

The rolling chair is as much a part of the Atlantic City boardwalk as the hard benches provided for the public. When in 1902 Mayor Franklin P. Stoy decided on a pageant of rolling chairs someone suggested that they place a pretty girl in each of the vehicles. The mayor retorted somewhat huffily: "Absolutely not. We are going to judge pretty chairs. *All* the girls are pretty. Who would dare to pick one out?" *

Beauty parades were held at Rehoboth Beach, Delaware, as early as 1880. Atlantic City's first Miss America Pageant was not held until September, 1921. "A bevy of beauties" in long bathing suits, stockings and hair bandanas marched along the boardwalk between Garden Pier and Steel Pier, and Margaret Gorman, a sixteen-year-old lass from Washington, D.C., was declared the first Miss America. In 1922 the event was opened by King Neptune emerging from the ocean, a part played by Hudson Maxim, the inventor of smokeless powder. Policemen, firemen, city officials and band members, each in a bathing suit, were allowed in the parade the following year, but of course none of them outshone the females. The parade was still an intercity contest in 1922 when fifty-seven entrants competed (only eight had entered the first pageant), and the out-of-state winner was

* John T. Cunningham, *The New Jersey Shore* (New Brunswick, N.J., 1958), pp. 149–50.

Mary Katherine Campbell, a seventeen-year-old brunette from Columbus, Ohio.

From 1928 through 1933 only one parade was held, and a city already suffering from the Depression lost money on this enterprise. The modern pageant, as we know it, was revived in 1936. Widespread publicity soon brought entrants from all the states in the nation, and, of course, made Atlantic City better known through the miles of newspaper print that followed first the state selection and then the national selection in Atlantic City Convention Hall. Such show-business personalities as Flo Ziegfeld, Earl Carroll, George White and producers of lesser rank took over the staging of the pageant. They were surrounded by beautiful showgirls who served as grand marshals. Television carried the pageant to an audience of millions who after 1955 awaited the moment of suspense when the toothsome Bert Parks as master of ceremonies sang "There She Is—Miss America." Perhaps he should have sung "Pennies from Heaven," for the girl who won the title was guaranteed during the following year at least $50,000 from various appearances arranged by a highly skillful business organization.

The sand dunes that Thomas Budd had bought for four cents an acre today sell along the boardwalk for about $4,000 a foot. Anyone who has ever played monopoly recognizes streets and avenues that belong to Atlantic City, a metropolis that specializes in wealthy monopolies.

10

The Begotten and Those They Beget

Exultantly Master Walter C. Letson ended the narration for the Class of 1909, Stelton Grammar School: "You know about the new schoolhouses which are getting redy for our use in the fall, and the graded schools which we are to have. You know that we have free text books, a supervising principal, a truant offiser, four examinations a year, and closing exercises in the Stelton church every June, followed by a long vacation. Don't you think 1909 is the best time of all?

No, I do not. I was not born until 1910 and my wife, Starling, did not grace this earth until mid-September of 1911, and New Jersey has not been standing still since the years unknown to Master Letson.

Sometimes Starling and I have fun recalling our experiences, some of which were parallel and some highly individualistic, during the years before we met and married. We belonged to an age, now too rapidly disappearing, when our grandparents were dominant members of the household. Starling's maternal grandmother was born in Berwick, England, and a framed picture of the bridge that crossed the river there made one think of "Flow Gently,

126

Sweet Afton." In the spirit of the early twentieth century she taught a little girl the things a little girl should know— sewing, embroidery, how to find pleasure in books. My own paternal grandmother, who lived to be a spritely eighty-three, grew up in a home where her grandparents recalled the incidents of the American Revolution, and she did not die until after World War I. She first aroused my interest in local history, and she liked to tell how Ulysses S. Grant and his family had summered in Long Branch; how James A. Garfield, struck down by an assassin's bullet, had gone to Elberon, then a part of West Long Branch, vainly hoping that the sea air would restore his health; and how she had met Woodrow Wilson when Shadow Lawn in Long Branch became the summer White House. She lived on the miserly pension given to widows whose husbands had fought in the Civil War, and when she died there was one dollar in her pocketbook. Since the others in the family knew how much I adored her, the dollar was used to buy me a child's collection of Bible stories.

Starling can remember when there were still canal boats on the Morris and Essex Canal, which was leased to the Lehigh Valley Railroad from 1871 to 1924, when it was abandoned. Starling received stern warning against ever communicating with the skinners whose mules pulled the barges, and it was sound advice, too, for they were a rough-hewn, profane and sometimes drunken lot. They cursed the muskrat holes in the towpath and the mischievous boys on the berm side (that is, the side opposite the towpath) who tossed pebbles at the mules, and most of all grew livid when they were made to drive a team of horses. The latter were far more sensitive than the mules and flared back when pebbles struck their ears. In very warm weather, they jumped into the canal for a swim, pulling the reins from the hands of the skinners, who became soaked trying to get them back on the towpath. For a time, amidst the swearing and the tugging, the situation would grow chaotic.

The Morris and Essex Canal ran from the Port of Newark to Phillipsburg, where a barge could be pulled across the Delaware River to join the Delaware Canal and thus travel southward to Bristol, where various feeder canals led to the Port of Philadelphia. New Jersey's other artificial waterway was the Raritan Canal. Tow boats pulled the barges, as many as a dozen at a time, through Raritan Bay to New Brunswick, where they entered the canal. Again at Trenton and Lambertville cables and feeder canals permitted the barges to cross to the Delaware Canal or the Delaware boats to cross to the Raritan Canal and proceed to the Port of New York or Philadelphia.*

So much of what we knew as children has disappeared: the kitchen coal stoves with their fancy nickel feet, which were doomed by the perfection of the gas and electric ranges; and shortly thereafter the maid or the couple who lived in were replaced by a multitude of mechanized gadgets for the convenience of the housewife in cleaning, washing, cooking and putting out the garbage.

In the years of our childhood cities were important centers of shopping and entertainment, but the urbanization of the State has brought decay and depression to these communities as surely as it has shrunk to a handful the number of self-sufficient family farms. It was an age of magazines such as: *American Girl, American Boy, Boys' Life, Open Road for Boys, The Saturday Evening Post, Country Gentleman, Literary Digest;* of pulp paper periodicals that featured Western, crime, and love stories; and of H. L. Mencken and the *American Mercury,* which specialized in picking on President Calvin Coolidge.

---

* A delightful book on the subject is *The Delaware Canal* (New Brunswick, N.J., 1967), written and illustrated by Robert J. McClellan. Its glossary of canal terms is superb.

The Roaring Twenties typified the giddy-headed sense of relief after the First World War; the flapper cut her hair and then bound her bosom so tight that she looked like a pole with a head; Prohibition brought the country's greatest drug craze with its bootleg whiskey and a crime wave which glorified the bootlegger and the bank robber. It was an age of the horse-drawn ice wagon with children climbing in back to chip off "suckers" on hot days; of the knife grinder, who carried his emery wheel by a strap fastened around his neck; of the junk man with his string of cowbells that disturbed the quiet of every graveyard he passed; of the hurdy-gurdy man with his organ, monkey and tin cup; of the roving bands of Gypsies and mothers who scandalized their daughters with stories of white slavery.

It was the age when Mr. Edison's phonograph made household names of Mr. Gallagher and Mr. Sheen; Mr. Edison's motion picture converted Mary Pickford and Rudolph Valentino into national love-images; when Mr. Edison's closed electric trolley was drafty in winter and his open trolley mosquito-ridden in summer. It was an age when children walked miles to school as long as the snow was not over their hips; when the flat cars of a traveling circus stood on a freight spur; when the town semipro baseball and football teams played in county leagues; and when every telephone wire was entangled with at least one kite.

New Jersey, according to the profile projected by its Department of Environmental Protection, is the most densely populated state in the Union. Yet hunters who occupy mountain lodges should not grow too inquisitive if they hear crashing noises during the night, for their visitor could be a two-hundred-pound black bear. Between three and four thousand white-tailed deer are killed each year by motorists, but the State's deer population is probably larger today than when the first white settlers arrived. In that part of Sussex County surrounding Hamburg there is an area of 200,000 acres of wilderness that is a haven for animals and birds. Four fifths of the original 300,000 acres of valuable salt marsh remain and are a home for more than three hundred species of birds, including waterfowl and wading birds. New Jersey streams are estimated to contain between fifty and sixty species of fresh-water fish. Small animals like chipmunks and raccoons not only abound in the marshes but also in the farmlands, where they can feed on wild fruit, raspberries and blueberries.

Starling and I as children both visited the beautiful falls at Paterson. We saw them not greatly changed from the time during the Revolution when Alexander Hamilton as an aide-de-camp to General Washington beheld "the astonishing depth of this receptacle [that is, the huge cavity below], . . . [where] the water neither foams nor forms whirlpools by the rushing current, but is calm and undisturbed." To Hamilton the enormous power of such falls once harnessed for industrial use was a memory never to be forgotten. In time the city of Paterson emerged: factories, largely silk mills, were the center for clattering trolley cars, stores, theaters and trains puffing columns of black soft-coal smoke on gagging pedestrians.

My father was not satisfied with making one crystal-operated radio set. He made two—one for himself and one for the remainder of the family. It was always a mystery to me how the thing worked, bringing in music from KDKA in Pittsburgh and all 103 ballotings of the Democratic political convention of 1924 over New Jersey's own station, WOR of Newark. In time we had a store-bought radio, filled with even more mysterious things called a condenser, tubes, a rheostat and wires that stretched like a spider's web.

The most sensational day on radio for me occurred one week before my seventeenth birthday in May, 1927. On this day a lanky mid-Westerner named Charles Augustus Lindbergh, in a monoplane called "The Spirit of St. Louis," attempted to become the first person to fly alone across the Atlantic Ocean. Day and night, or as long as any station was on the air, the radio carried bulletins of the progress of his flight: the rain at dawn had stopped when he prepared to take off from Floyd Bennett Field on Long Island; at 7:52 Lindy, the Lone Eagle, had waved his hand in a gesture of farewell, and his plane rolled forward; because of the extra fuel he carried, the plane had cleared telephone wires by not more than twenty feet before quickly changing course to avoid a row of trees.

Excitement rose in the voices of announcers as they supplied later details of how spectators had reported Lindbergh passing safely over Long Island Sound, Cape Cod, Nova Scotia. Then darkness closed in and there was nothing to do but to wait and pray for further good news at daylight. Next morning Lindy was reported approaching Ireland, and the drama was heightened by the sighting of "The Spirit of St. Louis" over Cape Valencia and Dingle Bay, Plymouth and the English Channel. The radio crackled with voices verging on hysteria—Lindbergh was over Cherbourg and then had landed safely at Le Bourget field in Paris after thirty-three hours and twenty-nine minutes.

At the realization of Lindbergh's mighty achievement, I felt as though I were walking on a cloud. Starling, approaching sixteen, pasted his pictures in a scrapbook. Most girls did. Within a fortnight there were at least a half dozen songs about "Lucky Lindy, up in the Air," and everybody danced the Lindy Hop. President Calvin Coolidge awarded Lindbergh the Congressional Medal of

Honor. At least seventy-five cities held parades to show their esteem for the Lone Eagle.

I was correspondent for the Associated Press when in 1929 Lindbergh courted Anne Morrow, the daughter of our ambassador to Mexico, but all I ever saw was their profiles as a limousine sped them through the gate to the Morrow mansion in Englewood. I was in college studying journalism in 1932 during the unhappy kidnapping and death of Lindbergh's infant son, when the couple lived on a secluded estate in the Sourland Mountains, and although our class was assigned to dig out the facts on the case, our total contribution to journalism and criminology equaled zero.

After conducting a number of important physiological experiments with Dr. Alexis Carrel of England, Lindbergh was assigned to making a report on the air strength of foreign nations. His belief that this country could never equal the air power of Nazi Germany earned him the ridicule of many, including President Franklin D. Roosevelt, and Lindy was so uncomfortable that he resigned his commission as a colonel in the Air Force. I remember how awed I was that in a single lifetime a person could be in turn courageous hero of the nation, the world's outstanding aviator, its most interesting lover, an object of universal mourning, a respected scientist and then virtually branded a traitor. But the ending was as happy as circumstances could permit. Lindy re-enlisted in the Air Corps after the attack on Pearl Harbor, served as research consultant and became a brigadier general in the Air Force Reserve.

Starling became my "consort" * in 1934, or the year following our graduation from the State university. Our first house was in Bound Brook on Chimney Rock Road near

* In New Jersey graveyards on eighteenth century tombstones the terms "consort" and "wife" were used interchangeably.

the base of the Watchung Mountains. Naturally one of our
first explorations was to Washington Rock above Dunellen.
This was the spot where, following the first winter encamp-
ment in the mountains around Morristown (1776–77),
General Washington came to gaze over the plains below
and wonder what was in the minds of the Hessians on
Staten Island and the British on Manhattan Island. On a
clear day the view is really marvelous: one can see for miles
over flatlands and rolling hills. There is a rumor of a second
lookout point closer to Blue Hills (Plainfield), where
Washington also was occupied in spying, but I never have
been able to find it, nor has anybody else I know. The source
of the story is Benson J. Lossing, who was a fine illustra-
tor and wrote millions of words about American history
but was often confused about facts.

There is a great deal of history of the mountains of
western Jersey that I do not know—the story of those who
made fortunes in iron mining, and the so-called pink-eyed
Jackson Whites who lived in the Ramapos—but then, one
of the eternal charms about the State is that there are
sufficient interests to satisfy anyone and still leave "special-
ties" for the next explorer. At Flemington, in Hunterdon
County, the residents are developing a center of colonial
crafts. Meanwhile strewn through the mountains—mountains whose names ring of Indian music, such as Kittatinny
and Watchung—are old towns, villages and hamlets that
are alive with the spirit and the appearance of colonial and
Revolutionary times. Now and then one stumbles upon a
lock or a tollhouse of the old Morris and Essex Canal,
historic prizes that should be jealously guarded. Even the
names of the towns have a cadence that is pleasant to the
ear. Pluckemin. Peapack. Flanders. Clinton. Pittstown.
Buttzville. Neshanic Station. Basking Ridge, where the
British captured the American General, Charles Lee, in his

nightshirt, and succeeded in getting his horse drunk after they chased him, bare bottom showing, to New Brunswick.

An explorer cannot always be sure that what he sees represents the true Jersey. A drive toward the famous Passaic Falls carries one through a valley that was once a ridge flanked on both sides by dense marshes: "5,000 [6,500?] years ago," or so Andrew Silk reported to the *New York Times* on August 13, 1972, "it was probably an island or a peninsula, and would have made an excellent camp ground." This discovery is the result of a series of excavations—scientists call them "digs"—made in the summer of 1972 by professors from Upsala College and residents of Livingston. The materials discovered belonged to that period in North American archeology called the Archaic Age (about 8,000 to 1,000 B.C.), when Indians were first learning how to cultivate the soil and hunt with bows and arrows. Relics and stones uncovered thus far verify these claims and also reveal that something new has been added to historical research. "There is an archeological thievery ring operating in northern New Jersey," Theodore Payne, in charge of the dig, has claimed, "so we must act with great caution, and keep the exact location of our dig confidential. Often professional bandits will pilfer relics and sell them to stores specializing in museum pieces or artifacts. There is a very popular bookstore in New York where you can walk up to one of the counters and buy spear points."

From spring through the early autumn the mountains are a paradise for tourists, picnickers, and that rather sizable group in New Jersey—those who enjoy dining out. In the spring the flashes of dogwood are a source of delight. The unfolding leaves seem to trace a green, gossamerlike canopy overhead. The sumac, which will droop with a purplish weariness when winter approaches, now shoots up through the skunk cabbage and poison ivy with the joy of a schoolboy awakening to his vacation. Fishermen in boots wade the mountain streams which the State stocks with trout, and someone must catch something, although I have not seen it happen in half a century. The ferns are spectacular in their lacy softness. In summer the green mountains have a breath-taking beauty, disclosing long vistas of rolling country that fade away into mists of blue and purple. In autumn the leaves are a brilliant mixture of reds and oranges and yellows and browns and greens.

My favorite spot in the mountains is Jockey Hollow, below Morristown, where Washington's army spent a winter (1779–80) worse than that experienced at Valley Forge. The National Park Service has done an excellent reconstruction of the soldiers' huts, the hospital and various other buildings, but to me the masterful stroke was preserving one road exactly as it was in Revolutionary times. It was along this road following that terrible winter, while Washington was in Connecticut conferring with his French allies concerning land and sea operations, that there were mutinies among the Pennsylvania and New Jersey troops. Somehow the army was pulled together and marched on to victory at Yorktown. Behind, they left wild violets pushing through the dead leaves of winter.

We spent summer vacations at Long Beach Island before it became such a popular spot. It was on the island that I taught our older son, David, how to fly a kite from a rod and fishing reel, an art that many observant children soon imitated.

It was there, too, that I became a lighthouse buff, and my heart always responded to the splendor of Barnegat Light, which stands at the inlet from the ocean to Barnegat Bay, one of the countless places from Maine to Florida locally known as the "Graveyard of the Atlantic." There is a claim that a hand-turned light stood by this inlet during the Revolutionary War. A permanent light at Barnegat, the fourth along the Jersey coast, was authorized by Congress in 1834, and $6,000 was appropriated to build a whitewashed brick tower fifty feet high. The metal parts were painted black and the whale-oil lamp did not rotate. A year after a more powerful beacon was installed in 1856, the whole tower toppled into the ocean.

The present lighthouse, constructed in 1858, was built with a Congressional appropriation of $60,000, and the Barnegat tower misses by only one foot being the tallest in the United States, an honor claimed by the lighthouse at Pensacola, Florida. The Barnegat Light tapers from ten feet at the base to eighteen inches at the top and is reinforced the whole distance by an iron pipe. A spiral staircase leads to the lamp, which used to throw a plane of light 163 feet above sea level. Henri Lepaute, a French expert—neat, formal, meticulous and fussy—was determined that the Barnegat Light should be his masterpiece. The lens assembly consists of 1,024 prisms mounted to form twenty-four large bulls-eye lens belts, each seven inches thick, eight feet in diameter and fifteen feet high.

Lepaute, convinced that no one in America could assemble such prisms, ordered them made at the renowned French furnace in St. Gobian. The bronze mountings weigh over five tons, yet the rollers are so perfectly balanced that the mountings will rotate at the touch of a little finger. The light worked on the principal of the grandfather's clock, but had to be wound every hour. It burned kerosene, generated 16,000 candlepower, and could be seen at sea from a distance of twenty-five English miles. The light flashed every ten seconds, indicating a latitude of 39 degrees, 6 minutes and 54 seconds, and a longitude of 74 degrees, 6 minutes and 1 second. The wicks varied in thickness from one inch to five, and the light tended to draw waterfowl, which were dashed to death against its outer surface. The government formally closed the light in 1927, replacing it with a lightship. But even the lightships are gone now, and New Jersey's coast is guarded by automatic buoys.

Legend indicates that when there was no lighthouse to safeguard this "Graveyard of the Atlantic," mules with lanterns had been led along the beach so that captains could route their courses by the direction of the island. But there were villains in every group, and in one instance they marched their mules around a haystack. A possible reason for this behavior in the opinion of Charles Edgar Nash, an authority on the island history, was to create the illusion of a lighthouse. In this case, Mr. Nash explains, "a lighthouse would serve as a warning from rather than an attraction to the beach . . . [and] it might throw a vessel off her course and result in a wreck farther up or down the coast."

The earliest known disaster was in 1705, when a sloop lost one of her crew and all of her cargo. But the wreck that lived on in the memory of the island's old-timers, which they told to their sons, who are probably repeating the story to a new generation, occurred on May 8, 1897. On this day the *Francis,* coming from California via Cape Horn, laden with salmon and the finest of wines, liquors and brandies, was driven by a fire on board to hug the coast and so was grounded on the bar off Little Egg Harbor Inlet. The crew of twenty-five was saved before the burning ship broke up, but the cargo was freely dispensed among the islanders. A 50-gallon barrel of sweet catawba wine was beached and her head knocked in. Some used tin dippers in helping themselves to this drink, and its mellow taste persuaded many to indulge in second and third helpings. Even clergymen and Quakers were part of the revel, for nobody seemed to realize that catawba wine had the kick of a mule.

The next two days, recorded Mr. Nash, were never equaled on Long Beach Island. With almost every wave other casks appeared—of port, madeira, sherry, champagne, burgundy, claret, moselle and tokay in addition to liquors and brandy. The village of Beach Haven was overrun to the verge of a stampede. Wagons and wheelbarrows carried off some of the casks, but enough remained so that one eye-witness exclaimed: "Pretty much everybody was a-feelin' good." Said another: "Crates floated by like schools of drumfish." One man smashed open a cask of port and handed it to passers-by by the pailful. Young ladies who never had touched alcoholic beverages indulged so liberally that they had to be guided home on their tipsy legs to bed, where they were told "to sleep it off." Many who tried to store the casks for later use by burying the barrels discovered, to their chagrin, that the metal hoops rusted and the wine seeped into the sand. But some made a very nice profit by selling nearly three thousand casks to a salvage company for three dollars a barrel.

Probably the most frustrated man on Long Beach Island was the stationmaster at Beach Haven. He placed a cask in a freight car and locked the door, believing his wine was as safe as though it had been stored in a bank vault. Disappointment met him when he returned for his prize. Someone had drilled a hole through the bottom of the car and barrel. Not a drop remained.

By the time our daughter, Meredith, arrived, we lived in Milltown. Although a housing complex has replaced the farm that once dominated the main street, the community has not lost its quiet, countryfied charm. It is situated on Lawrence Brook, a tributary of the Raritan, and its history probably started in 1816, when Jacob Bergen built a grist-mill there. In 1843 Christopher Meyer introduced "the industrial era to Milltown," and five years later there was a large influx of German immigrants. Among the mighty names in Milltown's history is that of André Michelin, whose rubber factory, we are told, "created an economic giant." * But the most heroic spirit of Milltown was a horse-and-buggy doctor named Norman N. Forney.

By chance one day Dr. Forney rode Mr. Edison's electric trolley from New Brunswick to Milltown. That Milltown had been served by Dr. Ferdinand Riva since about 1888 gave Forney discomforting reflections over whether the town could support two doctors, but when Dr. Riva departed in 1907, Dr. Forney decided to settle there. That Dr. Riva soon returned was not cause at first for rejoicing in the Forney household, but the two doctors shortly discovered that there was more than enough work for both of them.

An old-timer like Irving Crabiel remembers the Forney of those first years, kind, considerate, and greatly respected by the people. He had dark hair and brown eyes—"the dapper type," Mr. Crabriel said with a chuckle. Certainly Forney was not afraid of starting modestly. His first office was over a tavern, and the hallway he used for his reception room. More often Forney drove to his patients in a four-wheeled buggy, or a sleigh in winter. He covered a wide area, including Sayreville, South River, Milltown and New Brunswick and was known to treat as many as ninety patients a day.

No one could keep count of the number of miles he traveled; from day to day, he simply covered his rounds. Isinglass curtains pinned to the buggy frame helped to keep out the rain except when there was a squally wind from the northeast. In winter there was no choice but to let the snow pile up as deeply as it would, and sometimes, sighing, he had to climb out with a shovel to clear a path through a drift. His patients he kept catalogued in his mind, or, more likely, in his heart. When he reached a farmyard and some wild-

---

* H. Rodney Luery, *The Story of Milltown* (South Brunswick, N.J., and New York, 1971), pp. 34, 126ff. The author is especially indebted to Irving Crabiel for the insight he gave into the younger years of Dr. Forney.

eyed youngster dashed out with a cry of "You ain't got much time the way that new baby's whackin' Mom around," he would smile, pointing out that he was there when needed and his would be the whack that amounted to something, for it would start the new infant crying and breathing as it entered life. Sometimes he wondered how many babies he had delivered, but he lost track of those, too.

The influenza epidemic of 1918 was world-wide, and may have killed as many as fifty million persons. At least a half million of these victims lived in the United States. Dr. Forney would look down at the flushed faces of children and adults, knowing that no matter what he did, many were going to die. He had acquired by now an automobile and chauffeur so that he could cover his rounds more quickly and in between calls write his case histories. He was working around the clock, and his fatigue made him crotchety, his frustration quickened his temper.

At the turn of the twentieth century people were afraid of hospitals, and only when they feared death was near could they be made to enter such institutions. Dr. Forney conceived of creating his own clinic where he could offer for most ailments virtually complete outpatient hospital service. He was ready to open the doors of his clinic in the late 1920's, offering to take X-rays, perform laboratory procedures and make minor operations. His success could be measured by the rapid growth of his staff, which included two physicians, two registered nurses, an X-ray technician, and a registered laboratory technician. He was a doctor of the future, filling that interim before hospital insurance and Medicare changed the routine of medical treatment.

In his mid-sixties Dr. Forney accepted "semi-retirement" with almost boyish delight. He had already decided that he wished to fly a private plane, and mutual friends, who watched him training at the old North Brunswick airport, attest that he observed one of the bolder techniques of aviation: "coming in on a wing and a prayer." When our infant daughter required a tonsillectomy, the older man could not wait to try new procedures that he had learned through recent study. He did a fine job, too.

Our younger son, Bill, arrived after we had settled in our permanent home a half-block from where Miss Fillips had taught the Class of 1909 in Stelton Grammer School. Star and I had by then fulfilled Oscar Wilde's formula for a child's attitude toward parents—first to obey, then to question, and finally to forgive their frailties—and we await the time when those we begat will apply the same cycle to us and close what is so ominously called the generation gap.

Starling and I have been firm believers that part of the children's education should be seeing as much of the United States as possible, for a real feeling toward America cannot be gleaned through books. They have seen both the Atlantic and the Pacific, the rock-bound shores of Maine and the gentle coast of the Gulf of Mexico. No matter how far afield we have taken them there always has been a glow in their eyes when they have returned to New Jersey.

"We're home," they say.

And, indeed, they are.

ABOUT THE AUTHOR

Earl Schenck Miers was the author or coauthor of some sixty books, fiction, nonfiction, adult and juvenile. He is perhaps best known for his writings dealing with the campaigns of the Civil War, among which are *Web of Victory, Gettysburg,* and *The General Who Marched to Hell.* His latest work, published by Rutgers University Press in 1972, *Crossroads of Freedom,* is on New Jersey's part in the Revolutionary War. He was associated with the Rutgers University Press for thirteen years and served as its director from 1944 to 1949. He was an editor at the Westminster Press, Alfred A. Knopf Company, and the World Publishing Company. In 1953, he began to devote full time to his professional writing career. He died on November 17, 1972, shortly after completing *Down in Jersey.*

The text of this book was set in Caslon Linotype and printed by offset on P & S Special Book manufactured by P. H. Glatfelter Co., Spring Grove, Pa. Composed, printed and bound by Quinn & Boden Company, Inc., Rahway, N.J.